Contents

Section I: Miracle of the Timeline

Section II: Case Studies

Section III: Instructions

Peggy Pace, MA, developed the method of systematically using a timeline of real memories from a client's life for therapy. Her book and method are entitled *Lifespan Integration: Connecting Ego States through Time*. Lifespan Integration covers a much broader application than the Healing Timeline and is taught only to professionals with advanced degrees. Professional counselors are best suited to learn and employ her method. More information about Lifespan Integration and available trainings for counselors can be found at www.LifeSpanIntegration.com. Peggy Pace owns the copyright for the repetitive use of a timeline as developed for Lifespan Integration.

With Peggy's written permission, I combined the essential element of her discovery, the brain-changing use of a timeline, with Christ-centered prayer counseling, creating *The Healing Timeline: God's Shalom for the Past, Present and Future*. Thank you, Peggy.

Others made important contributions to the birth of this book. One friend, whom I lovingly thought of as Balaam's donkey, said to me, "Cathy, God told me to tell you to write your book!" It was the confirmation I needed. Another colleague, Rev. Terry Tripp, understood the power of this tool and arranged for the first group of lay counselors to be trained. Their success with the method spurred the vision to make the Healing Timeline available to more counselors. Trish Treece provided suggestions and book venues, reassuring me her prayer leaders were waiting for the book to be finished. Other colleagues whom I trained in the Healing Timeline reinforced the need for this material to be published. Their encouragement, suggestions, and success with the Healing Timeline are woven into the body of this text. Friend and reader-extraordinaire Debbie Hunter graciously added her editing skills to the final draft. And my sister, Doretta Hale, gave her input and guidance to, yet again, another one of my projects.

This book could not have been born without its doctor. Jamie Saloff is the book-publishing equivalent of the delivery room doctor who knew just what to do for this book to come forth. Christy Bishop prayerfully and skillfully designed a beautiful cover.

With Love and Blessings,

Cathy Thorpe, 2009

To my husband Craig
And our three children David, Tim and Kelly
"We love because he first loved us."
1 John 4:19

My friend and prayer partner, Corky Morse
Knowing you has changed my life.

Miracle of the
Timeline

One

Timelines Change the Brain

When I heard the news someone at church was mad at me, my stomach dropped. How could I be an adult fixing dinner for my family and feel like an adolescent whose world was crumbling from fear of being ousted from my social circle? Was it possible I could feel the grossness in my gut from junior high school three decades later? Being emotionally transported back into adolescence occurred a few times each year for me until it was permanently healed, in one session, with timeline therapy.

The Healing Timeline is a remarkable new Christian counseling method. As in all methods, it has a few similarities to previous counseling techniques yet is vastly different in other ways.

The Healing Timeline (HTL) works faster and differently than traditional forms of counseling and appears to rewire the neural networks of the brain, enabling rapid resolution of emotions tied to events and transforming them into more positive thoughts and behaviors. It is not an old method accelerated; it is a whole new approach to emotional transformation. We hypothesize the Healing Timeline brings about permanent changes in the brain. One client of the method said, "For years I have heard the back of my brain talking to me but I have never found a way to talk back. The Healing Timeline has given me a way to go back to the bad parts of my life and explain that it's over."

Healing Junior High Thirty Years Later

Using the timeline, a friend gave me the chance to go back to the years of junior high school and finally explain to my brain the bad parts were over.

Our family moved when I was in sixth grade. I left elementary school on Friday and was enrolled the next week in a junior high school a thousand miles away. Sixth-grade students were at the bottom of the social ladder and I was a neophyte in the world of adolescents—vulnerable prey for junior high sharks. Once a week or so, a supposed friend would share the gossip someone was mad at me and my stomach turned into the debilitating feeling of rejection. Unfortunately, this gut shot from junior high school seemed to operate on its own well after adolescence. No matter how many decades passed, several times a year an event would happen and my stomach automatically turned into the sour jelly mess of my youth. Although I was a fully functioning adult, my emotions had reverted on their own to 'Junior High Cathy.' The recent phone call about church was such an event.

To heal this repeated feeling, my friend asked me to remember being in junior high school. Doing so, I explained the worst of it to her, and she led me through a timeline of my life in which I pictured a personal memory from age 13, then a different memory for age 14, 15, etc., up to my current age. With a few other steps, we repeated this sequence three times over an hour. The final time I imagined myself in junior high school she asked if I felt any distress.

"No," I answered truthfully. The icky junior high feeling was completely gone. Although it had been present when we started the session, after three timelines the physical and emotional feeling had vanished.

"Then we're done," she cheerfully said.

That's it? I remembered thinking. *A feeling I have lived with for decades is gone – just gone?!*

My thoughts were swimming as I lay in bed that night. All the repetitions of the timeline left memories swirling in my mind, yet I felt very, very different and deeply relieved. No counseling session or inner healing prayer had ever been as effective as my experience that evening. I could feel emotional tectonic plates shifting. Not a trace of the frightened

Junior High Cathy remained inside. On a profoundly deep level, I understood I was no longer in junior high school. I was living as an adult and always would be. My brain finally got the idea junior high school was really over.

The next morning I felt even more like an adult inside. The interior shifts kept occurring and I knew something very profound had happened. I never again felt like Junior High Cathy. Not once, in five years, have I been emotionally transported back into the dreaded condition of being a rejected adolescent in an adult's body. On the few occasions when I have encountered the adolescent behavior of others, their responses did not recreate for me the earlier trauma. In each of those situations I felt and acted like an adult, and my stomach did not turn into the acidic glob of shame and isolation from my youth.

Peggy Pace is my friend who developed a specific process for repeating a timeline of memories in her therapy. The method is copyrighted by Peggy Pace and evolved into the book and therapy *Lifespan Integration: Connecting Ego States Through Time*. I was so impressed by my personal experience that I learned and began using her timeline method as well. The results were astounding.

My professional counseling practice has been informed by twenty years of Christian inner healing prayer. Because her method is copyrighted, I secured Peggy's written permission to combine the repeated use of a timeline with inner healing prayer. It is a simplified, specifically

Christ-centered version of using a timeline of memories in prayer counseling. The method described here is designed for lay and pastoral counselors.

To implement the Healing Timeline: *God's Shalom for the Past, Present and Future* (HTL), the spirit and image of Christ is invited into earlier memories. A prayer counselor then leads the client into a timeline of his or her life composed of real memories from their lifetime. The repetitions of the timeline prove to the client their hurtful experience is over. It is hypothesized that repetitions of the timeline create lasting, neural change in the brain. This hypothesis will be fully developed in a later chapter. By combining a timeline with inner healing prayer, the outcomes are exponentially greater than Christian talk therapy or inner healing alone. The method enables clients to really understand, on a mental and emotional level, that their old traumas and hurts are over. These changes appear to be permanent.

We are a composite of all our life experiences. When people fully understand on a mental, emotional, and spiritual level that the bad things in life are over, they are free to respond to today's challenges without the collective angst from yesterday's hurts. The case study *Pastors Need Help, Too* tells the story of a man with whom my prayer partner and I had used inner healing prayer and biblical counseling for several years. When we added a timeline to the work, he had lasting, life-changing shifts unlike anything we had seen before.

Rings of the Tree

One way to think about this collective description of ourselves is to consider the rings of a tree. People, like trees, are cumulative. When we grow, we do not stop being one age when we become the next age. An eight-year-old boy does not stop being seven when he turns eight. Instead, he becomes an eight-year-old with the thoughts, feelings, and experiences of the previous seven years. Humans are made up of all their years of life, just as a tree is comprised of all its rings.

We can look at the cross section of a tree and see the conditions in which it was grown. Fire, drought, good soil, and abundant rain produce very different growing conditions for the tree. In the same way, people carry inside themselves the conditions in which they were raised. Good or bad circumstances of their growing up years become the physical and emotional self that makes up their "human tree." Every thought, perception, and experience laid down in the human brain and body become part of the human self. When the Holy Spirit shines his light through us, he is radiating through every one of our rings.

Planted in our DNA, like the seed that becomes a tree, are our spiritual gifts, talents, and calling. While we are growing, these gifts and talents are developing inside us. The conditions in which we grow affect how well our abilities flourish. Like trees, we have a DNA directive for who we can become and our experiences in the world either enrich or hinder that development. Fortunately, we never lose the God-given creation of who we are even though cir-cumstances may stifle it.

This collective self, comprised of God-given gifts and life experience, is the person we carry through the world. When hurtful things happen, we can trigger a young ring from inside which informs us to run away or strike out with childish words. These thoughts and behaviors automatically activate when defenses are called for. A child who grew up in a violent home will have violent rings to draw from when facing the challenges of life. All rings can be triggered at any time. The neurons in these rings fire whether we want them to or not and inform how we respond to situations today.

Obviously, the structure of our human minds and bodies is infinitely more complex than the rings of a tree. Yet the analogy to us is clear. Even though we were created in our mother's wombs by a perfect God (Psalm 139:13), we are also affected by our life experiences in an imperfect world. By going back and healing life's negative experiences in the rings where they occurred, we can open the way for more of the God-created self to shine in the world.

Current research is telling us the brain can rewire itself.[1] We believe timelines, as developed and copyrighted by Peggy Pace, cause the brain to wire early areas of the brain to more grown up parts of the brain, which results in spontaneous, more mature thinking. The wonder of the

Healing Timeline is that we can help people remember the earlier rings that comprise their lives, and then prove those years are over, opening the way to fuller, more empowered living.

The form of Christian prayer counseling described in this book is a quantum step forward in healing human life where it was wounded. It is not traditional inner healing prayer or another form of talk therapy. Through the methods described here it is possible for people to go directly back to the time in life where damage took place and permanently heal that ring. The steps provided here cause the changes to be long lasting, without strain or effort.

The Basic Steps

The Healing Timeline is comprised of three steps:

1. Clients present a current problem or situation to a counselor. The client and counselor ask God through prayer to lead them to a former memory that needs healing in order to bring relief to the current problem.

2. The client invites Jesus into the memory scene. The client listens and watches as Jesus intervenes and speaks into the situation.

3. After the internal interaction with Jesus, the counselor leads the client through a timeline of his or her life

consisting of real memories. The client nods when these memories are recalled and the timeline continues without discussion up to the client's current age. Seeing Jesus in the memory scene and repetitions of the timeline are alternated until no distress remains in the memory scene. Sometimes a cue sheet of memories is used to help clients proceed through the timeline.

By using these three steps of the Healing Timeline, a client can expect the emotional distress in a memory to fully resolve, even if the trauma was many years ago. In one session, clients can move from being very emotional about a remembered event to being objective and rational about the same memory. Their objectivity lasts and includes more adult ways of thinking about their current problem. Brain research over the last few decades bears support for this hypothesis. Several sessions using the HTL can completely resolve hurtful experiences which led clients to incorrect, negative beliefs about themselves. Other prayer counseling modalities have guided clients to envision Jesus in a memory. Biblical counseling has rightly instructed clients to think differently about themselves and their problems. Adding the timeline and removing the emotional charge of a painful memory can integrate Jesus' truth and biblical principles into the past, present, and future. Integration through the timeline is the quantum leap for healing.

Combined with Other Methods

The wonderful thing about this method is the Healing Timeline is a tool that can be combined with other counseling interventions. It is highly compatible with biblical counseling, inner healing prayer, and spiritual direction. When the HTL is used to lower the emotionality of a memory, the client can progress to forgiveness, deliverance prayer or problem solving from a new perspective. Because wisdom and internal resources spontaneously emerge through the timeline process, clients can naturally move into solving their current stressors from a rational, adult perspective. Clients find their current problems much easier to solve when they are no longer activating younger, wounded parts of themselves who hold erroneous beliefs and misconceptions. Generally, clients don't know their current problems have roots in hurtful memories, but when they heal former experiences, their current situations look radically different and they self-generate appropriate solutions.

An example of using the HTL with counseling prayer can be drawn from the teaching about the power of bitterroot expectancy.[2] This is the condition in which an individual's heart and spirit are tuned to expect certain behaviors from others based on his or her wounding. Through difficulty and trauma we form judgments about how life and others will treat us. The judgment becomes a vehicle for experiencing the very thing we have judged. Applying the Healing Timeline to this problem, we first show clients that the negative experience that caused them to judge is over. When the anger and hurt feelings have dissipated from the ring which holds the memory, it is easy for clients to ask forgiveness and repent of their judgments.

Developing this example more specifically, a thirteen-year-old girl who was sexually abused by her father would judge him critically. It is human nature for a hurt young girl to judge in anger when she is a child and thinks like one. Yet the power of her judgment would cause the girl to experience difficulties later in relationships with men. Like planting seeds in a field, the young woman would harvest negative qualities in her future relationships with men, depending on how she judged her father. Not only will she experience the fruit of her judgment, the thirteen-year-old ring inside her brain will fire when she approaches intimacy. When we consider people are a composite of their collective years, the ring in her life that judged men based on her painful experience is still inside the grown woman who is trying to form good relationships. The brain cells that formed her early opinions of men are still present within her adult, brain. Without knowing it, she can be divided within herself — wanting to move forward toward romance as an adult but having a thirteen-year-old ring constantly inform her about the reasons not to trust men. By using the Healing

Timeline we can integrate the thirteen-year-old anger and heartbreak before we ask the adult client to repent of her judgments and bitterness.

When we take God's *shalom* into the past, we are healing painful earlier years. This level of healing transforms our experience in the present. We create a different future for ourselves when abuse, neglect, anger, bitterness, rejection, and hurt are resolved and forgiven. Believing the truth about ourselves, instead of lies, leads us into a very different future. Past, present, and future can be redeemed through the Healing Timeline.

In summary, The Healing Timeline looks similar to other therapies with one exception—it offers resolution of the emotional distress that hooks individuals to a past trauma or way of thinking. Like other therapies, the Healing Timeline looks for the root causes of current problems in earlier years of life. When a related earlier memory is revealed through prayer, the Healing Timeline offers an extra step of resolution. After inviting Jesus into the memory scene, clients are led through a timeline of their lives comprised of real memories. Repetitions of the timeline resolve the emotional distress associated with the memory and enable clients to spontaneously think differently about themselves and others related to the memory scene. The new ways of thinking reflect Jesus' truth spoken into the memory scene, rather than the childish way of thinking that would have originally been in place. The major advancement with this therapy is the apparent outcome that repetitions of a timeline from a memory scene will permanently alter the way the memory is understood. The theory behind this perspective will be developed in Chapter Three.

The purpose of this book is to provide an overview of the Healing Timeline and equip pastors and Christian lay counselors with the necessary tools to implement it in their corners of the world. Very specific directions and worksheets for using the HTL are provided here, as well as information for workshops in the Healing Timeline.

The second half of the book contains case studies providing examples where others have used the HTL in a variety of circumstances with life-changing results. Pastors, inner healing ministry teams, and individual lay counselors have used the HTL to move clients beyond anything they have ever seen in Christian counseling.

Throughout the book I refer to the person who receives the Healing Timeline as the client. Alternative words that could be used are prayer counselee or simply counselee. Variations on counselee seem a bit cumbersome when writing about prayer counselors and prayer counselees. To avoid confusion, I simply refer to the one administering the Healing Timeline as the counselor and the person receiving the ministry of the Healing Timeline as the client. By using this term, I am not implying any kind of professional relationship which might be associated with the term client.

As a young woman, I believe God showed me that I

would be involved in his ministry to "proclaim release to the captives.... to set at liberty those who are oppressed, to proclaim the year of the Lord's favor." (Luke 4:18). The Healing Timeline is part of the ministry God has given me to share with others. The Healing Timeline releases people from the oppression and captivity they carry within themselves. Long after our difficult experiences are over, we carry within our minds and bodies the thoughts, emotions, and fears that hold us captive. Releasing them through the Healing Timeline brings freedom.

I express deep gratitude to Peggy Pace who granted written permission for the use of her copyrighted timeline to be combined with Christian prayer counseling. Her method is taught to professional counselors only and has a much greater application than the Healing Timeline. The HTL method applies only to specific, remembered events. It may sound strange to add such a qualifier when considering memories, but some people have been traumatized so deeply they do not remember their traumas, yet they know something very painful happened to them. Others were traumatized before age two when concrete memory begins. Therefore, experiences that can not be remembered, or predate age two years old, are not suitable for the Healing Timeline. Yet there are many, many situations for which Christian pastors and lay counselors can use the power of the timeline to bring freedom to others.

Two

Talking or Timelines: Ted's Story

For decades, psychologists have suggested people's lives are influenced by their upbringing and history. Something about this proponent seems true; therefore, clients have been led to delve into their histories to understand the roots of their behaviors. Since people are a collection of their life experience, it does seem natural to look earlier in life to see where a problem started and how it influences behavior today. Another way to think of the "collective self" is to consider our lives like a continuous pipe: a section gets added each year and Christ's living water flows through us. When we hold a hose in our hand and the water isn't flowing, we look along the hose to see where the problem is occurring. Similarly, when we have trouble with the flow of our lives, it is reasonable to look for solutions in the past. Discovering the origin of a problem might bring greater understanding to the client, but is awareness sufficient to change the situation? Even with greater understanding, very often clients must constantly work to apply the new ways of thinking to old problems.

Trying to solve a problem decades after it occurred is like a plumber identifying a leak under the kitchen sink but making the repair on the outdoor hose. Yes, both places involve plumbing, but where does the intervention meet the problem? Some counseling methods have given clients a greater understanding about their problems, but the Healing Timeline can give them resolution where their problems began.

The Healing Timeline can significantly shift the role of talking as the primary method of change in Christian counseling. Many clients are very experienced at recounting the details of their painful childhoods, going from pastor to prayer counselor looking for relief. Biblical counsel and insight is imperative to help people achieve healing. Now the Healing Timeline can augment good pastoral therapy with brain-changing, emotional relief. The conversations that follow the HTL are very different than the conversations people have before they experience repetitions of the timeline. After the Healing Timeline, people talk about their problems from an adult perspective rather than the emotionally activated perspective of an earlier section within themselves.

Ted's Story

Ted's story further introduces the Healing Timeline and its application to many who have talked about their problems but not experienced sufficient relief. Ted is a client who had spent years talking about his emotional problems. Something very serious had occurred in his life and no matter how much he talked about it or how many groups he joined, he still had not found the healing he was seeking. His wife was threatening to end the marriage if he didn't get over his problem. Like others, Ted had received very good talk therapy and biblical counseling from his church over the years, but it wasn't until he experienced the Healing Timeline, and healed some earlier "rings in his brain," that he was able to understand and apply the concepts he had been taught.

Ted came to see me after praying God would show him some way to resolve his ongoing problem. In a chance conversation, a business associate mentioned his great outcomes from experiencing the Healing Timeline. Ted later told me, "That friend's story was the answer to my prayers. I know God brought me to you."

In our first session, Ted, age 59, recounted the many years he had been in counseling to get relief from a trauma he experienced 22 years previously. As a young professional man he traveled quite frequently. He was an outgoing, generous person who loved to help others. On one of his many trips he met a woman in a city where he often traveled. Over time they developed a romance, got married, and had three children. Ted continued to travel as his career developed and together they enjoyed raising their three daughters.

Ted and his wife Leah were actively involved in a church where they developed friendships. Their closest friends were Samantha and Jim. Ted appreciated the support they gave to his family while he was out of town and he reciprocated serving them whenever he could. Among his many talents Ted was mechanically gifted. He helped Jim with car maintenance on the weekends and had been the "right-hand man" during Jim's home remodel. The two families often spent holidays together.

In our first session together, Ted reported that his biggest problem was anger and debilitating jealously. He had been to other counselors about this problem and had recently been through an anger management course. He reported, "Believe me, I know what I'm supposed to do, but when other men get too friendly with my wife, I lose it. Then we go home and argue. My wife says she might leave me if I can't get over myself, but nothing I've done helps me get this under control. I can't stand it. After what happened with Leah, I'm a wreck."

Ted continued with his story. When his three girls were entering their teens, Ted came home from a business trip and found his daughters alone at home. "Mom has left," they cried. All of Leah's belongings were gone from the bed-room. As the story unfolded, Ted discovered his wife Leah and his best friend Jim were lovers and had moved away to start a life together. Leah began divorce proceedings and was not open to counseling or reconciliation. Jim also divorced his wife Samantha, who moved out of the area.

Ted was shocked and devastated by the end of his marriage. He said, "I gave so much to both of them. Jim was my best friend and I helped him whenever I could. Leah never gave me any sign. The weekend before they left, the four of us had a wonderful dinner together and I helped Jim fix his car. Even the girls say they didn't have any idea." Ted began to cry. "I know I'm overly jealous of my second wife, Cynthia, because of what happened 22 years ago. She says I don't trust her and I don't trust our friends. She's going to leave me, too, if I can't get over this."

In the years following his divorce from Leah, Ted married Cynthia. They had two children. Ted told me he had prayed for a faithful and loving wife, with some very specific qualities, and God answered his prayers. "I know God brought Cynthia into my life," he said. "It was almost a miracle the way he brought us together. She has never given me any reason to mistrust her. We've raised all five of the children together. I love her and I don't want to lose her. If I can't get over this jealousy, I don't know what will happen."

Ted was clearly in anguish over his situation. He had

tried very hard to follow the anger management steps and other advice he had received in counseling, but he was not experiencing relief from his jealousy. Since 22 years had passed since Leah left, Cynthia expected him to get over it and trust her. Ted agreed with Cynthia, and could cognitively understand why he should trust her and their friends, but he couldn't convince his heart to completely let go of its suspicions.

I reassured Ted he wasn't crazy and I was very confident he would experience significant change with this problem after a few sessions using the Healing Timeline. I explained to him his brain was something like the rings of a tree, growing a new ring for every year. At age 37, when Leah and Jim betrayed him, Ted's brain "logged in" the emotional devastation. He had mental, visual, physical and emotional recall associated with those years of loss. Even though he went on to live another 22 years and married a faithful new wife, Ted's brain and body were holding the memories that first registered the shocking event when Leah left their family. The fact it was so shocking compounds how deeply impressed into his brain the memory became. Expecting himself to simply get over it was not realistic since he was unconsciously triggered when similar situations occurred. Ted worked to control himself when his emotions got activated. I understood why he couldn't completely move on even though he had learned coping tools through anger management. Specifically, the part of his brain that learned the anger management method at age 59 was probably not well integrated into the part of his brain that held the trauma from 22 years ago.

Ted understood my analogy of the tree rings and agreed something like I described felt true inside him. Yet he didn't see how he could change this internal structure given how hard he had already tried. I reassured him the Healing Timeline would reach back into those "rings" holding the trauma from 22 years ago and permanently heal it.

"Something has to," he said with a sigh.

In preparation for the next session in which we would use the HTL, I asked Ted to write down a memory for each year of his life, encouraging him to use neutral memories if possible. Neutral memories are preferred, but the significant part of the timeline is to recall actual events that occurred in each year of life. Having them written down makes it easier to move through repetitions of the timeline. Ted agreed and we arranged for our next session one week later.

Ted arrived at his second appointment with a written cue list of his life. At my request, the list began at age two. Some memories were, "age four: first tricycle, age five: started kindergarten, age six: sledding during Christmas break, etc." His cue sheet had a memory for each age of his life up to the present.

To begin our session, I asked Ted to say a prayer giving God permission to go anywhere in his conscious or subconscious mind to accomplish healing. Ted chose to pray this out loud and I followed with a prayer asking God to guide our session. I had an idea about which memories in Ted's life would be related to his jealousy problem, but I have learned over the years to withhold my assumptions. It is better to trust the Holy Spirit, so I asked Ted to pray that God would guide us to the right memory for healing his over-reactive jealousy, the first step in using the Healing Timeline.

We waited quietly for a few minutes. With eyes closed, Ted said, "I can see myself walking into the house after my business trip and seeing the girls in the house. They have been crying and I can tell something is really wrong. That's when the oldest one said to me their mom had left and wasn't coming home."

I coached Ted to picture the scene vividly in his mind and then imagine Jesus in the scene as well. With eyes still closed, Ted said, "I can see Jesus putting his arms around the girls. Jesus is crying. He's sad, too."

"Is Jesus doing or saying anything else?" I asked.

"Not really," Ted replied. "I can tell he wants to comfort all of us. I'm basically in shock. I can't understand what the girls are telling me because it's unbelievable."

Ideally, the client would be able to see and hear Jesus interacting in the remembered scene. Occasionally in the beginning of the process the client is not fully able to see or sense Jesus' words and actions. Ted was emotionally frozen when he first remembered the devastating scene during our session, so I gently suggested a realistic, truthful comment Jesus might have said. I asked Ted, "Can you imagine Jesus saying something to you like, 'This is over?'"

Ted nodded affirmatively. As our work progressed, Ted was able to discern Jesus' words and actions himself. Until that time, I suggested simple, helpful phrases. I was doing my best to hear the Holy Spirit as I tuned into the scene as Ted described it.

"We're going to prove this is over with a timeline," I continued. Since this memory occurred at age 37, I began with the timeline cue from age 38. "Remember at age 38 when you went to your daughter's sixth grade Parent Night alone," I read off the cue sheet.

Ted nodded and wiped away tears.

"Remember age 39 when you let the girls get a dog."

Ted acknowledged again.

"Age 40, your friends gave you a birthday party…

"Age 41, you met Cynthia…"

After each cue, I waited until Ted gave me a signal he had remembered each memory after I read it. We continued through the timeline until we reached his current age of 59. At his present age, I asked Ted to open his eyes for a brief break.

He said, "I had other bad memories that came in, as well. I thought I would not get over that." He started crying and rather than pursue a conversation with him, I asked him to remember the memory scene again. "I can see it."

he continued to cry. "It's awful. I can feel my stomach as if someone just kicked me."

"Bring Jesus into the memory scene again," I directed.

"He's there." Ted's crying increased as he vividly recalled the events and emotions of the day. He was not able to identify Jesus' words again, so I gently prompted, "Imagine Jesus saying to you, 'This is awful but you'll make it through this. Here's the proof.'"

We proceeded directly into the timeline again. I gave him the first cue at age 38 and waited until he acknowledged the memory. He continued to wipe away tears as we went through the timeline but was a little calmer when we reached his present age. Opening his eyes, Ted said, "You know, I think that was the worst day of my life, but a lot has happened since then." We talked very briefly about some of the ways his life developed after that terrible day and then I asked him to return to the memory scene.

Even though he had been quite emotional a few minutes before, Ted did not cry when he visualized the scene for the third time. This is very typical of the Healing Timeline process. A memory can be very upsetting in the beginning of the session and virtually not at all upsetting by the end of the session. Noticing this progression, Ted remarked, "I guess I didn't know I had been holding so much grief about that day."

"As you are remembering it this time, what's the main feeling you're aware of now?" I asked.

"Anger," Ted answered. "I am really mad. I'm furious with Leah and I would love to beat up Jim! I can't believe my best friend did this to me. Or that Leah would leave the girls..."

After Ted invited Jesus into the scene again, we waited briefly to see what Jesus would say or do. Ted said, "I can see Jesus there but I can't hear him."

"Do you sense it's okay with him that you're mad?" I asked.

"Yes, somehow I can tell it's all right with him. He understands the pain I'm in."

"And here's the proof it's over," I said again, and then guided Ted through another timeline. Even though I used the cue sheet to lead Ted through his ages, he had spontaneous memories of times he was very angry, including the divorce with Leah and their custody problems.

After the third timeline, Ted said, "Wow, I guess I've been a pretty mad guy. No wonder I overreact to Cynthia. Have I been carrying this anger around the whole time?" he asked incredulously.

"More or less," I answered. "It's been sitting in one of those 'rings of the tree' in your brain, pretty much untouched. The fact that it brings up so much emotion when you remember it lets you know how buried, but alive it is as a memory."

We had time for one more timeline before our session ended, so I asked him to remember again when he walked in the door and found the girls crying.

"Oh, I can see it all right."

"What's the main feeling now?"

"Still anger," Ted answered. "Not as much as before, but I can feel the anger when I see this image. I feel sad, too, but I probably feel the anger more right now. Leah wrecked our lives by running off like that."

"Bring Jesus into the memory," I gently guided.

"He's there."

Ted said, "Now Jesus is holding me and I'm letting him. The girls are gone from the room and I'm alone with Jesus. He's saying things to me like, 'I never planned for this to happen' and 'I love people so much I give them free will. Leah and Jim exercised their free will.' He's telling me things really will get better. After the timelines we've done I can almost believe him."

I guided Ted through the fourth timeline and we closed our session. He was very tired from the emotional and mental work he had been through. His anger had subsided greatly by the end of our time together and we scheduled our next meeting.

"Any homework?" he asked.

"Just rest," I instructed. "You have done a lot of work today and your brain is reorganizing itself. Take care of yourself."

We began our third counseling appointment a week later by debriefing the previous week. Ted said he was tired for a day or so after our last session but then noticed some changes. He said, "I was a little less jealous around Cynthia this week and I had some thoughts I've never had before. I know this is going to sound strange, but it actually occurred to me that Leah and Cynthia are two different people. Just because Leah did something, doesn't mean Cynthia will do the same thing. I had a little more self-control in situations that might have bothered me before. Cynthia noticed I was calmer."

"I'm not surprised," I said. "It's normal for people to be tired after the timeline, but then the brain begins to give them new, helpful information. I think that's what you experienced this week. What are the main feelings you have now when you think about the memory scene of coming home from a business trip and finding the girls alone and Leah gone?"

"It's definitely different," Ted replied. "I can see how I contributed to this problem. I was gone a lot and I was a pretty selfish guy. I thought I was doing the best for my family by working so hard, but I can see that Leah was lonely. I was lonely too, but I didn't have an affair."

"Right," I validated. "You're beginning to see how a situation like this is very complex. It has many facets, all of which we can heal through the timeline."

"I hope so." Ted sighed. "I think the main feelings are regret and loss…grief, I guess."

I coached Ted to visualize the scene again and bring Jesus into the memory. He reported he could see Jesus in the memory scene and I asked him to pay attention to Jesus' actions or words.

"We're in the kitchen now," Ted answered. "We're sitting at the kitchen table talking 'man-to-man.' I can tell he has mercy for me but he's also honest about the part I played in our break up."

"How does that feel?" I asked.

"It feels good to be honest," Ted replied. "Jesus is speaking the truth but he's also kind. Looking at the scene now I can see how I contributed to the problem. I couldn't see it then, but with Jesus there I understand a lot more about what happened."

"And it's over," I added. "You did the best you could do and it's over."

Ted released a huge sigh and said, "That's true. I did the best I could. Occasionally, my dad was violent with my mom. At least I didn't do that. I didn't know how to earn a living on the road and keep Leah from being so lonely. I wanted to die back then when the break up happened."

We moved into the timeline and I read the cues from Ted's memory list. He nodded when he had a memory associated with each age. As we reached his present age of 59, Ted opened his eyes and said, "Some positive memories showed up in the timeline also. I started remembering times when I helped others and wasn't selfish. I wasn't a total failure. I gave a lot to Leah and my family. We were both ill-equipped to make the marriage work."

Each time we returned to the memory scene, Ted's feelings had shifted and were gradually becoming less painful. At the beginning of session three he felt grief and loss about losing Leah and the marriage, but also appropriate self-awareness about his role in the break up. During the session, he moved into feelings of regret about his upbringing and other ways he contributed to the difficulties in the marriage. For each feeling he identified, I asked if he could imagine Jesus saying some phrase that validated Ted's feeling and reassured him it was over. By the end of the session we had used the timeline four times. Ted was tired again but relieved. He could see that he and the girls had weathered the worst storm of their lives, good things had come out of the emotional storm, and God had led them into a current situation in which they were all doing well. He had gained a lot of insight about his own jealous behaviors and the emotional triggers rooted in the time when Leah left him.

It is common and realistic for this level of emotional resolution and self-awareness to emerge after only two sessions using the Healing Timeline. It was not necessary for me to give Ted the input that he was a major contributor to his marriage ending. By using the timeline, this awareness emerged after the feelings of shock, anger, and grief were resolved. Because the timelines always become spontaneously more positive as they are repeated, Ted also received the benefit of positive self-awareness regarding his strengths, coping skills, and obvious maturity that followed this difficult time. Growing awareness and emotional maturity also emerge between sessions as the timeline work continues to integrate into a client's life.

By session four, Ted was beginning to see his life from a new perspective. He reported being significantly less jealous when Cynthia interacted with other men and she felt emotionally closer to him. She felt the freedom to move closer to him in their relationship because he was reacting less. I asked Ted to reflect on the break up with Leah. He quietly took an internal inventory and said, "It's fine. When I remember the day Leah left I don't get any emotional distress about it. I understand it's really over. I wish I could have done it differently, but I know I can't. That life is in the past and I'm living a good life with Cynthia. God has forgiven me and I've forgiven Leah and myself." Ted's emotional affect was congruent with his words.

"What about the jealousy problem?" I asked.

"It's a lot better," he answered. "It's not gone, but a lot better. Maybe I'll never get over it."

I proposed we could make some more progress on the issue and asked Ted to give God permission to take him anywhere in his consciousness or unconsciousness to further heal the jealousy problem. I waited quietly while Ted asked God to take him to a memory so we could do more healing (step one of the Healing Timeline.) After a few minutes of silence Ted said, "I can see myself as a three-year-old who has been shipped off to my grandparents because my mom had a new baby. I lived with my grandparents at least four months after my sister was born. They lived four hundred miles away from my mom. My dad was gone for military service."

I asked Ted to describe the scene to me. He explained that his grandparents owned a hardware store in a small town where they both worked every day. As a three-year-old, he was expected to entertain himself around the hardware store while they worked, or he was allowed to wander into other shops on the main street of their town. "I was starved for attention," he confessed. "I wandered down the street hoping I could get someone to pay attention to me." My heart felt the loneliness of his younger child-self and I marveled that once again the Holy Spirit had taken us to just the right place to continue healing his jealousy problem.

Moving into step two of the Healing Timeline, I asked Ted to bring Jesus into the scene as he was visualizing it. He could imagine Jesus sitting on the sidewalk with him outside his grandparents' store. "We're looking at rocks," Ted reported, "and Jesus is talking with me. I tried really hard to get adults to engage with me but Jesus is just sitting there, not in a hurry, and we are discussing the stones in our hands. I get the feeling we could do this all day and he would never leave me." I coached Ted to imagine Jesus validating how lonely it felt to be away from his mom and dad during that time and to see himself reflected in Jesus' eyes as the smart and lovable little boy that he was. In truth, he didn't have to work at being loved or devise any plans for getting people to pay attention to him anymore. We followed this conversation with a timeline, step three of the Healing Timeline.

Together we moved through this session as before. Ted shared the feelings he noticed each time he visualized the memory scene, and I encouraged Ted to sense Jesus' words of validation and support to him about those feelings. We followed the internal conversations with a timeline. In this session we were able to complete five timeline sequences. In the beginning, I read cues from Ted's timeline sheet but then asked him to think of a spontaneous memory for each age as the session progressed. In the early timeline sequences, his memories were somewhat negative, related to the lack of receiving enough attention throughout many years of his life, but as the session progressed his memories became more positive ones. He began to have many real memories in which he was well-loved and attended to by others.

Ted was a smart and athletic student who was very successful in his growing up years. He began to see himself as a capable, well-loved young man rather than the hurt little boy he had been when his mother had a new baby. This is typical when using the Healing Timeline. At the end of the session Ted was tired again and said, "Wow, I can see how this stuff really works. I had never associated my jealousy with that time in my life. My mom did the best she could during war time with a new baby and a three-year-old."

Ted began our fifth session by saying, "Attention-seeking has been so much a part of my life that I'm going to have to recreate myself if I let this go. I spend fifty percent of my life trying to get attention. Who would I be if I didn't work so hard to get attention?"

Ted was describing his insight, which resulted from the previous session. He was beginning to understand on a deep level that his life had moved on from the early years in which he saw himself as a boy starved for attention. Although I could not prove it, I suspected that his brain was rearranging itself and integrating new material (his current life) with earlier, painful memories. Once again, self-awareness was emerging after a session using the Healing Timeline.

During the fifth session, Ted and I again focused on the young boy who spent several months with his grandparents after the birth of his younger sibling. Ted asked Jesus to lead him to the right memory for healing and Ted remembered another scene from the months with his grandparents. He saw himself lying in bed at night wishing someone would come in and kiss him goodnight. He missed his mother's affection and closeness. He expressed the confusion, sadness and loneliness of a little boy who had to go to sleep on his own, wishing he were home with his mother.

Jesus was invited into the scene and comforted the younger Ted. After four conversations in the memory scene, and repetitions of the timeline in which the grown man occasionally wiped away tears, Ted reported the little boy from the memory scene was fine. "He's sleeping peacefully now. He understands he didn't do anything wrong and he wasn't really alone. His grandparents loved him very much and did the best they could. It was wartime and everyone worked really hard. My grandfather stayed late at the store and my grandmother took me home to give me supper and be with me in the evening. They both made sacrifices for me. When I was lying in bed alone she was serving my grandfather dinner. It's different when I look at it almost sixty years later."

I agreed.

In two sessions using the HTL process, focused on healing Ted's jealousy, he was led through prayer to memories of needing attention at a very young age. Neither he nor I would have deduced that his jealousy with Cynthia was directly related to his childhood need for attention when his mother had a new baby. Talk therapy might have ferreted out this connection, but only the HTL could reach back into the ring where the injury took place and heal it. In very few sessions, Ted's inappropriate jealousy virtually disappeared.

Ted and I met together a few more times, using the Healing Timeline in each counseling appointment. In the beginning of each session, Ted described the progress he was making through the HTL therapy and his current stressors. Each week, after a discussion of the current problem, we asked God to guide us to the right memory for healing and invited Jesus into the memory scene. We repeatedly followed the memory scene with repetitions of the timeline until the memory contained no negative emotion.

After a few months, Ted applied for a job which needed a doctor's recommendation. He made an appointment with the psychiatrist who had directed him into the anger management program. The psychiatrist interviewed Ted and gave him a personality test as part of his evaluation. Ted described the results of his personality test to me. Remarkably, there were no signs of anger problems. His test scores were positive for emotional stability and maturity. Through the interview, the doctor deduced that Ted was "clear-thinking and well-balanced emotionally." The doctor gave him high marks for being able to manage his emotions in the challenging situations that would be present in the job for which Ted was applying. According to the psychiatrist, Ted was an excellent candidate for the stressful but rewarding work. He also wrote, "whatever stressors were apparent before anger management seem to be resolved and are not prone to impair the candidate's ability to function." Before Ted used the Healing Timeline, the doctor told him he would always have the problem of managing his anger. Two years later, using the Healing Timeline, the same doctor rated him as mature and emotionally stable, able to perform well in stressful situations. Ted credited the change to the Healing Timeline.

The business associate who referred him to me also described Ted as significantly changed. They had worked together for years. After our few months of counseling, the business associate could not believe how positively different Ted had become.

As for the jealousy with his wife, Ted said, "I'm a new man. We're almost like newlyweds. I don't have the emotional triggers anymore and my wife can't believe it. Previously, she avoided situations in which we had to work together and now she invites me into her volunteer work. She keeps asking, 'Are you different because of the Healing Timeline or are you taking some kind of pill!?'"

He smiled at me and said, "You and I know it's the Healing Timeline. Thank you so much for helping me. I think everyone should experience the Healing Timeline."

I agreed again and we concluded our therapy.

Reviewing the Steps

In review, the Healing Timeline has three major steps. One, a client presents a current problem or seeks healing for a specific, remembered event. Two, the client gives God permission to go anywhere in the client's conscious or subconscious mind and asks to be guided to the right memory for healing. Three, Jesus is invited into the memory scene and speaks words of validation, truth, and the assurance that the difficult memory is over, followed by the timeline. This process is repeated until the memory scene produces no distress when remembered. In most cases, no matter how distressing a memory scene may be, the HTL will fully resolve the emotional pain associated with it. In the following chapter I will discuss why we suspect this occurs.

As clients move through the above sequence, their thoughts and feelings during the memory scene always shift. Generally, clients progress from confusion or shock to hurt, sadness, anger, grief, regret, forgiveness, and acceptance, including self-acceptance for their own poor choices that may have deeply hurt others. For some readers, it may seem inappropriate that clients would finally reach self-acceptance for their own wrong doing. I believe Jesus wants to heal all of us from our sins, those we inflict on others as well as sins that have been committed against us. The Healing Timeline creates a path for emotional clearing of all of our hurts, which opens the avenue for forgiveness.

Forgiveness

It may be noticeable that I did not urge Ted to forgive Leah and Jim in the beginning of our sessions together. Neither did I lecture him or give biblical advice or counsel. At some points in our sessions, I deliberately did not engage him in conversation that would have led into deeper discussions that might have been typical for traditional talk therapy. Instead, I kept returning him to the memory scene and timelines to eliminate stored emotion. The purpose of the HTL is to clear the emotional distress which clients are holding in their minds and bodies to make room for greater wisdom to enter. A heart filled with anger and resentment is not a readily open vessel for advice or teaching about forgiveness. Over our time together, because of Jesus' interventions, internal conversations and the timelines, Ted moved from anger, self-pity, and grief to acceptance, forgiveness and an awareness of his role in the break up of his marriage. Gradually, it changed his over-reactive jealous behavior with his second wife, Cynthia. If Ted had not moved toward forgiveness on his own, I would have encouraged him to forgive Leah, Jim, God and himself before our work was finished. Forgiveness is much easier to suggest and accept when the emotional stress of a situation is resolved.

Timelines, then Talking

The beginning of this chapter purports the Healing Timeline works faster than traditional talk therapy and employs a unique modality for creating change. Rather than talk about a situation, in the HTL process a counselor guides a client to heal hurtful memories through repetitions of the time-line. We hypothesize the timeline creates permanent change in the client's brain, resulting in new ways of thinking and behaving in current situations.

Conventional therapy involves talking with people about their problems, praying with them, giving them bib-lical counsel and encouraging them to change their lives through increased wisdom and insight. This method works and will continue to be valuable. It is an effective method, but it can also be challenging and lengthy.

What if we could accelerate the rate for emotional healing? Such a method would not take the place of pastoral counseling, inner healing prayer and spiritual formation, but it would give fast emotional relief, which would enable people to live their lives in new ways, easily integrating Jesus' truths into their lives.

Conversations are very different after the timeline work has been done. Many clients conclude the repetitions of the timeline by saying, "Now I understand why I've made the choices I have." Without exception, when asked about their presenting problem, either in the session or at a later time, clients report very different perspectives on their difficulties. Problems that seemed insurmountable at the beginning of a HTL session have obvious solutions after the timeline repetitions.

One woman who was very distressed by her teenage son's behavior said, after the HTL, "I'm going to go home and tell him that I will not put up with his inappropriate behavior. If he's going to keep doing it, he can live someplace else." The tone and resolve in her voice communicated strength.

As her counselor, from the beginning I wondered why she tolerated his rude and disrespectful behavior toward her. It would have taken a lot of talking over many sessions to convince her to set a boundary with her son. When the woman healed part of her childhood fear of abandonment through the timeline, she understood that she was the adult in the parent-child relationship and it was her place to set loving but firm boundaries with her son. Before the timelines, she was identifying with the child's position in the relationship. This way of thinking limited her ability to be in the adult role. After the Healing Timeline, our parenting conversation was very different as she clearly became the adult in the problem-solving situation.

Ted and this woman talked very differently about their problems after we used the Healing Timeline to heal the emotions involved in their stories. The Healing Timeline can pave the way to deeper, more insightful conversations than could ever occur without the emotional relief generated by timelines. When clients have talked about their problems a lot, like Ted did, the Healing Timeline is a welcome answer to emotional healing. It resolves life's problems along the continuum where it was broken, and that is something to talk about.

Three

Why the Healing Timeline Works

The repetitive use of timelines in therapy, as developed and copyrighted by Peggy Pace, catapults clients into resolution of traumas, enabling them to rapidly access more positive memories and emotions to replace their negative ones. Over several sessions, clients experience rapid and lasting healing of emotional problems. Yet at this point in its development, we have not proven with the scientific method why the Healing Timeline works. We could interview clients, though, who have had their lives changed with the method, and they would tell us they have experienced accelerated and permanent healing through timeline counseling. Unfortunately, we do not have brain images or detailed research projects to support the claim that repeated timelines produce brain change and therefore lasting behavioral and emotional change in clients. It would be helpful to have the kind of research that supports our experience. Instead, we have the collective experiential data from clients and a large supply of current information about the workings of the brain. These two elements combine to support the hypothesis that repeated timelines cause neural changes in the brain resulting in clients' new thinking and behavior.

Neuro-plasticity

A major shift has taken place in recent years regarding the scientific understanding of the brain. For decades we were taught the brain grew throughout childhood and then was "set" like a hardboiled egg. Once the brain was set, nothing could change its essential wiring. It could lose or gain a few synapses over the years, but it was considered developed by early adulthood with not much opportunity for change. Now we know through current, extensive research the brain is the opposite of a hard cooked egg.

The first tenet behind the hypothesis that timelines change the brain is the clear understanding the brain is a living, changing, plastic, collection of matter that is being renewed and changed until the end of life. *Neuro-plasticity* is the term scientists have given to the brain's impressive ability to change its structure and function in response to experience.[1] *Neuro* is for the neurons which are the nerve cells in our brains and nervous systems. *Plastic* means changeable or modifiable.[2] Therefore, neuro-plasticity is the condition which enables the brain to modify itself in response to various stimuli.

Neurons are the cellular components of the brain. Each neuron has three parts. The cell body sustains the life of the neuron and contains its DNA. Branching out from the cell body are dendrites, treelike branches that receive input from other neurons. Finally, the axons are living cable of varying lengths that carry electrical impulses toward neighboring neurons. The microscopic space between the axons and the dendrites is the synapse.[3]

Brain Rules, by John Medina, describes the interior world of the brain in simple metaphorical terms. By using everyday metaphors, Medina illustrates the complex functioning of the brain. It is a good resource for understanding brain function and how the brain constantly changes in response to various forms of input. The plasticity of the brain means change is possible throughout a lifetime.

Brain research reveals humans can rewire their brains as needed. Sharon Begley's book, *Train Your Mind, Change Your Brain,* describes how the "brain can undergo wholesale change…that the brain is capable not only of altering its structure but also of generating new neurons, even into old age. The brain can adapt, heal and renew itself after trauma…."[4] One of many ways the brain can change is by intentionally redirecting thinking. Brain imaging maps can be made of these changes.[5] They show long-standing,

physical changes in brain areas after test subjects intentionally worked to change their thoughts or after spontaneous
change was generated in the brain due to stroke, injury, or
disability. The brain's capacity for renewal and re-genera-
tion is remarkable and is at the center of the hypothesis that
timelines change the brain.

Rewiring

The second contributing dimension to the workings of timeline therapy is Hebb's hypothesis originated in 1949. It is a
central maxim of modern neuroscience which states, "neurons that fire together, wire together." Our mental activities
actually cause changes in the structures of our brains; not
only what we think, but how we think, as well.

In layperson's terms, Hebb's hypothesis means neurons activating at the same time increase their connection
with one another. Repeatedly activating neurons together
strengthens their connection. Norman Doidge, MD, states,
"When we say that neurons 'rewire' themselves, we mean
that alterations occur at the synapse, strengthening and
increasing, or weakening and decreasing, the number of
connections between the neurons."[6]

In 2000, Eric Kandel won the Nobel Prize for proving when people learn something, the wiring in their brains
changes. "He demonstrated that acquiring even simple
pieces of information involves the physical alteration of the

structure of the neurons participating in the process. Taken broadly, these physical changes result in the functional organization and reorganization of the brain. This is astonishing. The brain is constantly learning things, so the brain is constantly re-wiring itself."[7]

Given the plasticity of the brain and its capacity for rewiring, the theory behind the Healing Timeline is the concept that difficult, emotional memories can be wired to newer parts of the brain that have developed since a difficult memory was stored. In other words, by taking someone through a timeline of his or her life, we can rewire the neurons holding a painful memory with new data stored for each year of the client's life. For example, it is suggested a memory stored from 1949 will be rewired with information from 2009 when a client is taken through his or her lifetime with brief memories.

In the case of Ted and his over-reactive jealousy, it would appear neurons holding memories of age three when he was away from his mother for several months and age 37 when his first wife left him during an affair were rewired to neurons up to age 59. The observable changes in Ted's thinking and behavior would support the supposition that brain rewiring took place through the timeline. When Ted was three he thought and reasoned as a child (I Corinthians 13:11). At age 59, Ted was able to understand the circumstances that took him to his grandparents for several months. When these two ways of thinking were combined through the timeline (neurons that wire together, fire together), Ted had an organic new understanding of himself that was more adult than his childhood mind could grasp. After the time-lines, when his wife Cynthia interacted with other men, Ted automatically understood with his adult mind that he was no longer a child being displaced in a woman's love.

Ted does not have to work at remembering the new concepts because they appear to have been rewired in his brain. The anecdotal evidence we have seen in HTL therapy supports this hypothesis. Also, Ted's work in the anger management class was not completely successful for creating change because it did not get wired into the neurons that triggered his jealousy. The jealousy triggers and the new information about anger management were held in separate parts of the brain, which were not integrated with each other.

Integration

Integration is the third component in the hypothesis that repetitions of the timeline change the brain. Dr. Daniel Siegel, MD, states, "Integration is mental health."[8] In order to function at its best, a person or system must have inte-gration of it various components. There is no upward limit to how much complexity a system can tolerate as long the system is well integrated. In other words, it does not matter if a system has a few parts or many, many parts. The quality of the system depends on how successfully the parts work together — how well they are integrated.

For example, a university with 35,000 students can function as well as a university with 2,000 students if the parts of the system are working well together. If a university's admissions office admits the number of students who can be accommodated in classrooms, dormitories and cafeterias, then the system can function well. If one part of the system does not have integration with the whole, the functioning of the whole system can be shut down. An admissions office that allowed 10,000 students to attend a university designed to handle 2,000 students would create a problem for the whole university. That university system would have many students (an aspect of complexity), but not integration.

As Dr. Siegel states, the principle of integration applies to mental health. If all the "brain departments" do their job, the brain is fully functioning. Mental dysfunction occurs when one part of the brain holds a trauma or memory in a non-integrated way. Dr. Siegel suggests a lack of integration contributes to mental and emotional impairment not simply because the content or amount of data is too great, but because the brain 'departments' are not working together.

His theory is validated by the outcomes from the Healing Timeline. Occasionally clients who are trying to resolve a current problem in their lives will be taken back to a very distressing memory through the prayer process.

When clients are shown that even their most difficult memories are over through the timeline, they appear to integrate and resolve past traumatic events. Their symptoms of distress drop away after several repetitions of the timeline and do not return. We believe these results occur because the timeline integrates the painful memory, which was not fully processed. If someone was in shock from a severe event, his or her brain may not have finished its work. Repetitions of the timeline appear to aid clients in finishing the processing of their traumatic events. In other words, integrating the painful memory.

An example of the power of integration can be seen in Marie's story. A neighboring boy sexually abused Marie at ten years old, and like many children, she was warned by the perpetrator to never tell anyone about the abuse. Marie remembers lying in bed at night, feeling like a bad girl, and being too ashamed to tell her parents the secret. This molestation occurred during summer break from school.

When we used the Healing Timeline to integrate the abuse memory, Marie identified a connection she had never made before. The school year that followed the summer of abuse was a terrible year for her academically. Within the first few weeks of school, Marie's teacher told her parents not to expect anything from Marie. The teacher described her as "distracted, in her own world, and unable to learn anything." Previously, Marie had been a very social and successful elementary student. The abuse over the summer was diminishing the workings of her brain and reducing Marie's capacity for learning and socializing. We could guess her brain was trying to come to terms with the trauma, which affected other forms of processing.

Marie said, "I struggled academically after that summer and I never knew why." We integrated the memory fifteen years later and Marie noticed an improvement in her work performance. When one part of a system is not able to function well within the whole, the whole system is affected.

Another way to think about the neural integration would take us back to the rings of the tree analogy mentioned earlier. Although far more complex and sophisticated, the brain, like a tree, starts out in a fairly undeveloped state and progresses through life by adding layer upon layer of self-generated material each year. Trees grow a new ring for every year of life and human brains develop new neurons and complex neural networks every year until the end of life. As layer upon layer of brain matter develops, more and more neural networks are laid down.

If we think of brain layering like the rings of a tree, it is possible for one ring of the tree to not have any connection to or awareness of another layer. It is highly likely that material laid down in one set of neurons at one age will have no direct relationship with material laid down in neurons from another age. The pre-frontal cortex of the brain (center front) can access all regions within the brain, but various sections, or rings, often do not have any connection to one another.

Ted's experience in anger management is an example of layers being separated from one another. The memory and anger associated with his first wife leaving him got activated in his brain when his second wife Cynthia interacted with other men. The coping strategies he learned in anger management 30 years later did not appear to have a direct, causal effect on the neurons which held the memory of his wife's affair. Using the tree-ring analogy, we could think of them being in separate rings that developed thirty years apart. The pre-frontal cortex had access to each piece of information, but the separate memories did not influence each other in a way that helped Ted reduce his jealousy.

The hypothesis behind the Healing Timeline is that systematically asking clients to recall real memories from their lifetime will fire neurons holding the memories. Repeating the timeline will build a neural connection between memories, or "rings." which were previously unrelated. Given the vast complexity and layering of the brain, it is very likely portions of the brain holding certain neurons are dissociated or disconnected from other neural groupings, even though they can both be known through the pre-frontal cortex. When neurons have joined together into new neural pathways, clients will understand their former problems are over and they will think and feel differently. When experiencing the Healing Timeline, clients often spontaneously say, "Wow, the child in the memory had no idea I had grown up!" How could the child not know the client was an adult when they shared the same brain? The answer: the younger memory was held securely in the "ring of the tree" where it developed and did not have access to rings that developed later.

Connecting the neural groups through a timeline could be likened to the sandbag brigade that forms when a community is faced with a flooding river. When the truck arrives with sandbags, helpers form a line from the truck to the water's edge. The closest workers reach into the back of the truck, grab the bags of sand, hand them to the next person and so on until the sandbags are stacked against the river to protect its banks from overflowing. When the truck is empty, the sandbag brigade has done its job.

The sandbag brigade is metaphorically like clients using the timeline to integrate a difficult memory or joining separated rings of the tree. By activating neurons in a memory, then connecting a bit of the memory to the next year's neurons in the brain, and to the next year, etc., we suspect a neurological path forms from the memory to the present. According to Hebb's hypothesis, neurons firing along the years are wiring together. Eventually, like the truck whose contents once held a pile of sandbags that got transferred to the water's edge, the isolated contents of a memory will be reconfigured and connected to more recently developed parts of the brain. The neurological path created through this process is strengthened with each repetition of the timeline.

God's Perspective on Integration

A pastor trained in the Healing Timeline shared a dream that highlights God's perspective on integration. A woman dreamt she was standing in a barn. The barn was dark and the doors throughout the barn were locked. The dreamer had a feeling she should go into the house and leave the barn, but she could not force herself to move in that direction.

After meeting with her pastor one time, the woman returned and told of a new dream. She said, "I had a dream this week which was like my dream from ten years ago. I was in the barn again but this time it was light. Jesus was standing in the middle of the barn. Around the center of the barn were doors, which were unlocked. Behind the doors were children of different ages and I sensed they were all me. Once again I was directed to move toward the house. When I awakened I heard a word repeating over and over in my mind—Integration."

Continuing, she said, "I had no idea what integration meant or why it was associated with the dream. I looked up 'integration' in the dictionary and found out it has something to do with personality and wholeness."

The pastor carried the meaning further, explaining to

her, "The word wholeness is sometimes derived from the same root word shalom as used in Mark 5:34. Shalom is the Hebraic word meaning to be made whole, be as you were intended." The pastor assured the dreamer she could be helped to achieve integration and wholeness, which would lead her into peace. Together they began the work of the Healing Timeline, a method designed to create integration.

Summary

This chapter provides simple descriptions for considering the brain. A great deal of information is available today on the sophisticated workings of the brain and the most rudimentary concepts have been presented here. These descriptions are not intended to be a complete thesis of brain plasticity and renewal. Instead, the discussion of these brain concepts is intended to support the hypothesis that the brain can be rewired through the Healing Timeline to create mental, emotional, and behavioral change for clients. Although much could be written and discussed about the brain, a few basic concepts have been outlined for the purposes of understanding the workings of the Healing Timeline.

In review, three main principles underlie the hypothesis for change through the Healing Timeline. First, the brain is a living, changing organism that creates new neurons throughout life, contrary to the previous theory that the brain became fairly solidified once it reached adulthood. This adaptive, changing nature of the brain means it can be rewired and literally restructured through intentional thought changes. We believe repetitions of the timeline are one intentional thought method that changes the brain in an enduring way.

Second, the changes created by the timeline most likely occur because neurons that fire together wire together according to Hebb's hypothesis. Applying this principle to the timeline, we hypothesize neurons from one period of life are systematically fired along with neurons from other years of life when clients are guided through a timeline of their lives. Neurons from separate years are wiring together when clients are prompted to remember the years of their lives. Repeatedly firing these neurons together strengthens their connection until a new way of thinking develops regarding former problems. Circumstances, which provided negative emotional triggers at one time, lose their emotional charge when tied with more adult, up-to-date thinking through the neural reconnection.

Third, integration is mental health. All parts of a system must be working together in order to have the optimum functioning of the system. When one part of the brain is overloaded with emotional material, the whole brain system and its functioning is reduced. In order to return the brain to its optimal level of functioning, difficult or dissociated "rings" must be re-integrated with one another. This is accomplished through the timeline. If a difficult experience occurs at a young age, the brain may be holding the information out of consciousness or in an isolated, protected way. Joining the neurons that hold the memory to years of life that have occurred since childhood, integrates the information and increases the brain's overall functioning.

Mental integration, neurons firing together, and the living, changeable nature of the brain combine to create lasting emotional change through the Healing Timeline. It is suggested these results occur because the brain is actually rewiring with repetitions of the timeline. The results from the Healing Timeline reflect a level of emotional healing we have not seen before.

The timeline method of counseling is different than talk therapy because it does not rely solely on a client's intellectual understanding of issues, but rather goes back to the source where beliefs were first developed and gives clients the opportunity to rethink what they know and believe. The timeline integrates the new ways of thinking. All people process emotional distress with their young minds by assuming the challenges they face have something to do with themselves. This developmentally appropriate self-centeredness leads to wrong conclusions when things go awry. We can change thinking that developed in childhood or previous "rings of the tree" by integrating the thoughts, feelings, and beliefs that were formed in earlier years.

By imagining Jesus in a memory scene, and adding

truth followed by the timeline, we can help individuals heal on a profound level. Jesus has no limitation of time. When he goes back to enter a memory scene with a client and speaks the words of healing, clients are able to grasp their experiences with new understanding and form new conclusions about themselves. We hypothesize the timeline integrates this work and causes new neural pathways to be formed. Anecdotal evidence supports the hypothesis. The Healing Timeline appears to create integration and integration is mental health.

The Case Studies section that follows gives several more examples of the ways in which the Healing Timeline is changing lives.

Case Studies

Four

Pastors Need Help, Too

This case highlights the benefits of adding a timeline to traditional inner healing prayer. My prayer partner and I had prayed with Brian, a beloved pastor, several times over a few years and in each session we had followed the guidelines of traditional inner healing prayer. He appreciated our ministry and felt helped by our efforts. After learning about the use of timelines to lower the emotionality of a memory, we combined the two modalities for the first time with this pastor. The outcomes astonished all three of us.

The week after our prayer counseling session using the Healing Timeline, Brian called to say he was experiencing major emotional shifts unlike anything he had experienced with us before. He explained that his thinking was very different and it was clear to him what course of action he needed to take. He was energized for taking those steps.

Previously, we had coached him to take some specific steps after our prayer times, but he was usually unconvinced or reluctant to follow our guidance. After the HTL, he took action from his own new perspective and we were delighted to encourage him in those steps.

After our first HTL session with the pastor, we combined the timeline with prayer counseling in various formats. Sometimes a client would present a work or relationship problem as the reason for seeking prayer counseling and in the midst of telling her story would mention abuse from her childhood. After the prayer asking God for guidance, we would often begin by healing a client's abuse with the Healing Timeline as the precursor to solving the current work or relationship difficulty. All forms of childhood abuse influence an adult's way of thinking. We found that by listening for God's direction and healing early trauma, clients were better equipped to successfully resolve the problems from their work and personal lives.

The following case example is Brian's story from our first session in which we used the Healing Timeline in prayer counseling. As the son of a pastor, Brian had been raised in the church. His father spent his full career in pastoral ministry, but was also an alcoholic who barely provided for the needs of his family. They lived in a poor neighborhood and struggled in every way. Brian was the oldest of seven children and provided the primary male leadership in his family. His mother relied on him heavily for decision-making;

he was the surrogate father figure for his younger brothers and sisters. By age ten he was babysitting his family while his mother worked.

As a grown man, Brian had a dynamic ministry and a deep, personal relationship with the Lord. His mother and grandmother had taught him to hear the voice of God. Brian took his relationship with God very seriously and desired to obey Jesus in everything he did. He was a highly respected teacher and leader in his community and the nation, often teaching throughout the world. It was a privilege to be with him for inner healing prayer. Although he was the client when we gathered for prayer ministry, my prayer partner and I sensed God's favor and presence with him in such a deep way we were in awe when our sessions ended. Brian knew the scriptures, was a gifted preacher, and he manifested an uncommon anointing from the Holy Spirit.

On this particular time he joined us for prayer ministry his father was in the hospital 40 minutes away, possibly facing the end of his life. Brian was deeply disheartened when we began our time together. His shoulders sagged and his voice was heavy. Brian wanted to follow Christ in his actions toward his father, but he said, "I just can't go down there and play some pastoral role at my father's bedside." He sighed and dropped his head in defeat. We understood that he was referring to the years of neglect, abuse, abandonment, and humiliation he had experienced throughout his father's life. "I can't bring myself to rush down to the hospital and stand there with my brothers in some emotional scene that is total hypocrisy." We felt his deep pain. "I can't go and clean up one more mess," he said.

Brian clearly wanted to follow Jesus in his life, but he was not able to overcome the years of chaos and shame his father had brought into the family. When we had prayed with Brian previously, we had been led to painful, heartbreaking memories of life in his childhood home. Regarding the visit to his father's possible deathbed, it was clear Brian could not motivate himself to do what he considered the right thing because he was weighed down by the years of drama and disappointment with his father. I wondered if the man of God before us who had ministered so powerfully to many people would be able to act on his faith in this personal situation. I felt compassion for him, yet worried about the session in front of us. What could we do that would help him when he was the heartbroken son, not the pastor, at someone's side?

As we always do, we began our prayer counseling session by asking God to guide the session and lead us collectively wherever he chose to lead. We asked Brian to give God permission to go anywhere within his consciousness or unconsciousness during our session and he painfully obliged. Brian asked God for direction and we waited silently in the heaviness. After several minutes we asked, "What are you sensing? Where is God leading you?"

Brian opened his eyes and described a memory we

had previously visited in inner healing prayer. The incident occurred when he was 11-years-old. He had come home from school and found his mother distraught. She was bereft from the discovery of another one of her husband's sexual affairs. Brian tried to persuade her to leave his dad and she finally agreed. For the rest of the afternoon Brian worked urgently to move the family's belongings into the car so they could leave before his father returned home.

After everything was loaded and Brian was getting the kids ready to leave, his Dad came in from work. Angered by what he found, he berated Brian and cornered his mom in the house. Brian went outside while his mother and father argued for two hours. He could hear their yelling and accusations from the driveway where he was shooting baskets alone. At the end of the shouting match, Brian's mother came out of the house and told him to carry everything back into the house; they were staying. Defeated, the 11-year-old obeyed. Brian lay in bed that night thinking he was a failure.

I remembered the previous session in which we had been led to this memory. We had not learned about the Healing Timeline yet and it had been very, very difficult for Brian to forgive his father. At that time, we asked him to forgive his father, not from an emotional perspective, but as a matter of obedience and choice. The request for forgiveness was followed by twenty minutes of sighs and silence. Brian was not being stubborn; he was grappling with the years of heartache, betrayal, and his own failure to make things better for the family as a boy. Eventually, he conceded and we led him through a grudgingly compliant forgiveness prayer. It was less than buoyant and Brian left that session still discouraged.

In the current session, I was surprised we had been led to the same memory again. Rarely did we revisit a memory scene after the client had re-witnessed it with Jesus present. The Holy Spirit can always be trusted, though, to guide clients to the right memory for healing. Our current session with Brian was no exception.

When Brian described the memory in this second session, I anticipated another challenge in which we would eventually ask him to forgive his offenders, knowing he would have to overcome years of emotional obstacles in order to follow Jesus' directive for forgiveness. Our session turned out very differently though because we combined a timeline with inner healing prayer.

Brian told us again about moving the family's belongings into the car and his dad coming home right before they left for safety. In his memory, Brian saw himself outside playing basketball alone while his mother and father argued. We asked him to invite Jesus into the memory.

Brian envisioned Jesus being with him in the driveway, next to the loaded car. I asked him if he could imagine Jesus saying something like, "You did the best you could.

This is over." Brian nodded he could imagine Jesus saying this to him. Before we went any further in the memory, I asked him to go through a timeline, beginning at age twelve. Brian got a spontaneous memory at age 12, then I asked him to think of a memory for 13, etc., until we reached his current age of 45.

When we reached the end of the timeline, I asked him to view himself again in the driveway with Jesus. Instantly, he said, "That's right. There really was nothing I could have done about it." A new level of awareness and relief were evident in his voice.

"What's happening now?" I asked.

"I'm still devastated," Brian replied. "I'm leaning against our car with all the stuff inside and I'm trying to take care of our family. I was pretty sure my mom was going to go back with my dad and I felt hopeless. I worked so hard to get all that stuff out of the house for nothing. We had been putting up with my dad's drinking and affairs for so long…"

"What's Jesus doing?"

"Looking at me with compassion and love. I can tell he's really sad about what my dad is doing. He did not want this for our family."

"What is he saying?"

"He's explaining to me I was just a kid. He's telling me he loves me and it won't always be like this. He has plans for me and I'm suppose to focus more on getting to know him."

"How does that make you feel?"

"Like I'm important. Not just because I can help my family but he's actually interested in me."

"Can you imagine him telling you this is over and you're not stuck here anymore?"

"Yeah."

"Let's go through another timeline and prove it really is over."

I guided Brian through another timeline. Occasionally, he wiped away tears as we progressed through his ages. When we reached his present age, Brian said with a sigh, "I have spent my whole lifetime cleaning up after my dad and taking care of my siblings. Sometimes they resent it when I get involved now, but a couple of them are having trouble like my dad did. I've spent my whole life taking care of people."

"Do you think God is calling you to do that now?" we asked.

"Not really," Brian responded. "They are all adults and my dad is 72 years old. He and my mom have been doing this for over 50 years, I don't think I'm going to change it now. My dad has stopped drinking and they are doing better, I guess." Brian's words reflected new insight which became apparent to him through the timeline. "And my mom has finished school and has a good job," he added. "Things are a lot more stable for her."

"Let's go back and finish helping the 11-year-old in this situation," I coached.

Brian saw himself again as the 11-year-old boy in the driveway.

"What's happening now?" I asked.

"I'm relieved to know it's over but I'm also sad. I worked so hard to get my mom and us kids out of there and now she's going to stay with him again. I feel like a failure."

"Would you invite Jesus in again?"

"I can see him go into the house and talk to my mom and dad. They stop fighting because Jesus is there. It shocked them that Jesus walked into the living room. He explains to them they are hurting the kids and each other. He says some other things to them I can't quite hear, and then he comes back outside to talk to me.

"He says again there really isn't anything I can do about their situation. He understands I want to help. He's telling me I'm a good kid. It feels so good to have someone talk to me like this. I can tell my shoulders are relaxing and I'm beginning to feel good because someone is relating to me. He's telling me I'll grow up and do important things for him, but for now he wants me to be a kid. I look in his eyes and see amazing love."

"Can you imagine him saying, 'You are not a failure. You are an amazing kid in an impossible situation.'?"

Brian nodded, acknowledging he could imagine Jesus saying this to him.

"And can you imagine him saying, 'It's over'?"

"Yes and I'm glad." Brian sighed, visibly releasing his shoulders and settling into a more restful posture.

"Think of a memory at 12, 13, 14…." I directed.

At the end of the timeline, Brian was awestruck in a positive way. "Man, I can't believe it. I have been trying to clean up other people's messes my whole lifetime and most of the time it doesn't work."

We confirmed he had been trying to overhaul his situations as a boy by helping others and he was using that same strategy as an adult. Brian was still trying to help his mother, father, siblings, and others, whether they asked for his help or not. He was often frustrated by how hopeless his efforts appeared and he had been baffled by the resentment he occasionally encountered.

"One thing you were doing as a boy," we offered, "was trying to make things better for yourself. You wanted to have a better home life so you were doing everything you could to fix the situation for your mom. Can you see now as an adult how impossible that was?"

"Without a doubt," he quickly responded. His body language had shifted from the defeated man with whom we started, to a more relaxed, relieved guy who was making sense out of his history and linking it to his present behaviors.

"Let's go back to the memory scene one more time."

Brian readily agreed.

When we were back in the memory scene for the fourth time Brian saw his younger self shooting baskets with his basketball.

"What's he feeling?" I asked.

"He feels like a kid," Brian responded. "Like a kid outside shooting hoops after school. He knows there's nothing he can do about his mom and dad's problems, and Jesus has promised him things will get better."

"Any distress?" I asked.

"No," he easily quipped.

"Can you bring Jesus into the scene with you?"

"Oh yeah," he replied. "He's playing ball with me."

"What would Jesus like to tell him?"

Brian pondered for a minute and said, "This kid needs to know he has a lot of talents and he should spend more time working on them than hauling his family's stuff into the car."

"Can you imagine Jesus telling him that?"

"Yeah," Brian replied. "But Jesus is saying it while we play ball. It's cool, like a dad and a son. My dad never played ball with me but Jesus is hanging out, telling me stuff like that. I really like it."

Brian's voice and demeanor matched the warm, casual

scene he was describing. He smiled while he visualized the memory scene for the fourth time.

Because Brian reported no distress in the memory scene and his emotions and body language were consistent with his report, we moved into the final timeline.

I asked him to think of a memory at 12, 14, 16, 18, 20, etc., choosing to use only the even-numbered ages because we were nearing the end of our counseling time and he was reporting no distress. The purpose of this timeline was to primarily connect him to his adult self, rather than to leave him focused on the younger scene. We wanted him to walk out of the session feeling very adult.

At the end of the timeline, Brian shook his head in a positive form of disbelief. "Wow," he said slowly. "That was amazing. I've never seen before how that was a turning point for me in my self-esteem. I felt like such a failure when my mom agreed to stay. I thought I had a good plan to get us out but she changed it. At the time, I didn't even know how significant it was. Looking back at it now, I can see the beginnings of depression. I felt badly about myself when all that happened and it had nothing to do with me. I didn't know it at the time, though. I guess I thought it was my fault we didn't leave. I don't know how I came up with such an idea."

We confirmed all children relate everything in their world to themselves. It is the appropriate, ego-centered nature of children. Because Brian was feeling badly when the incident took place, he internalized the negative feelings from the situation as reflecting something about himself personally. The pattern of personalizing the situation is true about all children and often true about adults. Brian assumed there was something wrong with him because things went awry. It would be totally outside the realm of a child's mind to think, *My mom and dad are troubled adults. They are having a tough time coming up with good solutions to their problems. I'm sure this has nothing to do with me.*

As we were debriefing the prayer counseling session, Brian began to laugh. "I was a good kid," he said, " but I guess I wasn't God."

We joined him in his laughter.

"Would you be willing to forgive your dad?" we asked.

"Absolutely!" came the instant reply.

We asked Brian to visualize Jesus standing near the cross after his resurrection and imagine taking his Dad into the scene as well. When Brian nodded he had the scene in his mind, we guided him to say anything he wished to his father. We told him honesty was required and he did not need to edit out anything that seemed 'un-Christian.' Brian chose to speak aloud to his dad. He told of his hurt, anger, disappointment, and desire for them to have a relationship. He spoke of his needs as a child to have a dad take care of him and the family. He wanted a dad to play with him.

Brian concluded by saying, "I guess you did the best you could and I forgive you."

We guided Brian to ask Jesus for forgiveness regarding the wrong ways Brian had judged his father and the vows he made as a boy. Vows are very powerful determinants and we wanted to see Brian set free from the inner resolutions he made during those young, stressful years. Earlier in his life, Brian had falsely determined he was a failure. Although he was a very successful man, he carried the childhood belief about failure in his heart and it continued to resonate through him. Brian asked Jesus to forgive him for the lies he believed, the vows he made, and the accusations he formed against his father. Scripture says, "Do not pass judgment, that you may not be judged; for the way you judge, you will be judged and with the yardstick you measure, you will be measured" (Matthew 7:1). We did not want to see Brian walk in the path of his father by holding judgments against him even though his father had clearly been in the wrong.

When considering the memory scene we had visited, it may seem odd Brian had a reason to ask Jesus for forgiveness. Did he do something wrong by attempting to help his mother escape an alcoholic, unfaithful husband? No, Brian as a child was clearly a victim in the situation and did not do anything wrong, but he childishly made determinants in his heart about his father which had the power to bear fruit later in his life. Only God is the appropriate judge of men and we are clearly admonished not to judge lest we experience the same problem we are judging. We wanted Brian to experience freedom from his past, not recreate it. We knew one important step toward that freedom was to seek God's forgiveness for any way Brian might have condemned his father or locked himself into vows.

After Brian had forgiven his father and asked for God's forgiveness, we asked him to describe the scene he was viewing. He told us that earlier in the scene his Dad had been standing beside him, but now he had stepped behind Jesus and Brian couldn't see him anymore.

We asked Brian to imagine bringing his mother into the mental picture. He visualized her standing next to him where his dad had been. Once again he spoke aloud, telling his mother of his heartbreak, judgments, childhood needs, and love for her. He spoke words of forgiveness to her. We coached him to ask Jesus and his mother to forgive him for the wrong behaviors and judgments he had made from his hurt, boyhood heart. After these words, Brian told us his mother seemed to disappear behind Jesus also, giving us the clue he had done the necessary forgiveness work with his mother regarding the particular memory we had worked on during the session.

Next, we guided Brian to forgive himself. He started believing he was a failure which began to bear the fruit of depression in his life. He judged himself as inadequate when he could not solve the problems from his father's drinking, affairs, and financial lack. When his mother reversed the decision to leave their home to escape his dad, Brian judged himself personally responsible for their failed attempt. Like all judgments, these beliefs had taken root and had been growing in his heart for many years. Although he was a boy, and it would have been impossible for him to resolve the family's distress, Brian had judged himself and he was in the best position to reverse the decision. We coached him in a prayer of self-forgiveness as he stood before Jesus in his imagination.

Finally, although it may seem odd, sometimes it is important to forgive God for events we have experienced. We asked Brian if he was holding any anger or judgment toward God for allowing the situation with his mom and dad to take place. He quietly searched within himself and said, "No, I don't think so. I know enough about God to believe this is not what he wanted. Sinful people make sinful choices which we all have to live with. God didn't do this to me. I'm not mad at him for it. Now there are a few other things I might need to forgive God for..." he said jokingly, and we assured him we would deal with those other things later.

When we closed our session, Brian was light-hearted and jovial. The strength he normally portrayed had returned and he did not look at all like the man who was feeling powerless to visit his dad in the hospital. The day after our session he traveled forty minutes to visit his father. He later reported it was the best conversation they had ever had between them. Brian was able to express some of the regrets he had about their relationship, and his dad, for the first time, was not defensive. The emotional shift inside Brian created an atmosphere where his dad could honestly speak about their problems without defending himself.

Two of Brian's brothers later came into the hospital room and together they developed a strategy regarding his father's medical needs. Brian reported the story to us saying, "For the first time in my life, I didn't have to be in charge of it all. It felt really good." This is a typical shift after using the Healing Timeline.

As mentioned previously, Brian was the first prayer-counseling client with whom we added the Healing Timeline to inner healing prayer. Before, we had also invited Jesus to replay the scene in Brian's imagination to reveal his truth and presence. The experiences were helpful to Brian, but at the end of each session it was painful and drawn out for him to consider forgiving his offenders. The stored emotion and cumulative heartache that remained made it almost impossible for Brian to forgive.

In the Healing Timeline session, we were led to Brian's childhood memory for the second time. The contrast was great between our first inner healing session with the memory, which required twenty minutes of coaching for Brian to reluctantly forgive, and the second session with the same memory, in which he was open and eager to forgive his parents and himself. His self-generated words of forgiveness in front of Jesus were honest and genuine. He exhibited none of the resistance we usually experienced from him. The difference between these two sessions was the Healing Timeline. Not only was forgiveness effortless, but also the insight Brian gained about himself and the situation was greater than anything we had seen before through inner healing prayer. Similarly, the changes he easily made afterward were greater than we had noticed from him following previous prayer counseling sessions.

Brian's first session with the Healing Timeline set the pattern for many of our healing prayer sessions. We began to use the Healing Timeline in other prayer sessions to help clients relieve the emotions tied to a difficult memory. After the emotion was removed from the memory scene, we followed with forgiveness prayers, deliverance, or problem solving. The work of the Healing Timeline made it much easier and more effective to move into the other aspects of prayer counseling.

Several years after his first session, Brian continued to show significant changes from our work together. We followed with other sessions that produced major changes in his life. He reports his relationship to his mother, father, and siblings have changed for the better and his own marriage has grown tremendously. He has greater insight about himself and he is able to evaluate when he is the right person to solve a problem or when he is overstepping his bounds.

The problem of over-responsibility has definitely decreased. Brian has deep appreciation for the prayer counseling and Healing Timeline and says, "It completely changed my life." He continues to seek out prayer counseling with the Healing Timeline and credits it with deep spiritual and emotional changes he observes within himself.

Five

War Trauma

These case studies speak to a tremendous need in our world: healing adults and children who have experienced war. A professional counselor should treat severe post-traumatic stress disorder whenever possible, but I have met several missionaries who deal with children whose lives were ripped apart by the impact of a civil war in a developing country. Resources for professional counselors are not available in remote villages. Although missionaries and outreach teams do not have the resources of a professional counselor, they can offer victims of genocides and war the loving presence of Jesus and show them, through the Healing Timeline, that their time in the war is over. This intervention may not be as thorough as might be experienced in a trained professional's office, but it is a step in healing the emotional and physical trauma people have experienced in war-torn countries. Ongoing trauma results when the brain of a war victim does not understand the war is over. The Healing Timeline offers children and adults resolution of their traumas by helping them integrate their horrific experience of war into the present, which is hopefully safer.

A missionary to Uganda cites an example, which underscores the perspective mentioned above. She spent three years counseling a young girl who was not able to learn due to PTSD from her parent's death in the war. After one session using the HTL, the fourteen-year-old girl came back and said, "This is really helping me." The missionary used the timeline with her for three more sessions.

On furlough in the United States, the missionary told this story. "A new team came to Uganda from the US and brought the Healing Timeline book with them. I read the book and decided to give it a try. I did not know if I was using it correctly, but when the 14-year-old came back and said she wanted to use it again I agreed. The four sessions using the Healing Timeline were more effective than the three previous years I had spent counseling her. That's when I knew there was something about this method."

Constance Hobbs, missionary to New Hope Uganda, said, "The four, one-hour sessions using the Healing Timeline were more effective than the three years I had spent counseling the 14-year-old girl. That's when I knew there was something about this method."

Rebels in the Congo

During the years the timeline method of counseling was being developed, a young man from the Congo was praying God would heal him from his war trauma before he graduated from college. Tresor was in the last year of his studies at Ozark Christian College in Joplin, Missouri when we met at a Christian counseling conference. He told me about his talk therapy experience in the US two years previously. Tresor hoped the counseling would cure his symptoms of post-traumatic disorder from the civil war he experienced in the Congo but, unfortunately, his six months of traditional counseling were not effective in resolving the PTSD symptoms. Yet he continued to pray for God to heal him. During our conversation I told him about the Healing Timeline. At the end of the conference he returned to Joplin to complete his senior year and we exchanged a few emails after our meeting.

In the spring, I invited Tresor to attend a Healing Timeline training. He traveled for a weekend to the Pacific Northwest, (USA), and as suggested, brought a timeline of his life to the workshop. On Friday night before the conference began, I suggested using the Healing Timeline for his war trauma. With his permission, I share the story of the one session he experienced at the conference and how it changed his life.

At fifteen years old, Tresor was at home in his compound when his father came home from work in the middle of the day to announce rebels had come to their village. Everyone was very frightened and Tresor climbed into his bed to shut out the noise and fear. Buried under the bed sheets, but unable to sleep, his stomach hurt every time he heard gunshots. Afternoon turned into evening and Tresor remained completely covered. When periods of silence came, Tresor feared the family dog would bark and rebels would burst into their home. The neighbor lady told his mother that the rebels were taking boys Tresor's age and forcing them to fight. Tresor had many reasons to be afraid. Throughout the evening the family prayed, Tresor hid, and darkness took them into morning. Occasionally, Tresor fell asleep during the night but awakened with pain in his stomach.

In the morning the village was quiet, but by noon the fighting was as bad as it had been the day before. Tresor's mother called him to the midday meal which he ate obligingly only to please his mother. When the noise arose in their compound, he heard commotion from the house behind theirs where a rebel had been caught. As they talked about burning the rebel alive graphic images filled his mind. Realistically, he feared that a rebel would burst through the door, kill his family, and take him captive.

Gunshots sounded throughout the second night.

The following morning, the radio advised villagers that the rebels were gone and they were safe to go about their normal lives. Tresor's father returned to work and his sister visited a friend. Tresor, though, was afraid to leave the family compound. He did not want to see the rebel who was burned alive.

Due to the rebel threat, the start of school was delayed for two months, during which time Tresor stayed near his home in the family compound. When his freshman year of high school began, Tresor did very poorly due to his post-traumatic stress disorder. He had been an outstanding student before the rebels entered his village, but after the trauma he was unable to succeed in school.

Tresor said, "When Christmas came, it was no celebration for me. I was still very sad and troubled." When school was dismissed at the end of the year, he still stayed inside the family compound. He failed school the second academic year after the trauma.

To begin our Healing Timeline session, I asked Tresor to imagine being in his house right before the trouble started. He said he could see himself at home when his dad walked in and said the rebels were in the village. "Can you imagine Jesus being there?" I asked.

"No," he replied.

I sensed Tresor was quite disturbed by remembering the scene, and I promised him it would different, forever, if he would be courageous and experience the Healing Timeline with me. We began the timeline. Because this was a very intense trauma that lasted for many hours, I used timeline cues from several time periods of both days and something for each day afterward for approximately the next week. Conceptually, this trauma was frozen in many segments, all of which needed to be 'unfrozen' through the timeline. Moving from age 15 directly to age 16, which is typical for the timeline, would not have incorporated enough of the traumatic frozen elements for healing. In the case of severe trauma it is useful to incorporate many cues near the trauma to fully resolve it.

Because Tresor could not see Jesus in the traumatic memory, I assured him the trauma was over and asked him to remember hiding under the bed clothes hearing gun shots outside. He acknowledged the memory and I moved onto the next memory of him lying in bed at night, fearing the dog would bark and the rebels would burst through the door. Then I said, "Remember sleeping very little during the night and having a stomach ache." Tresor nodded again and I moved through all of his cues up to his present age of 26 years old. Even though he could not initially see Jesus in the memory scene, I knew that within a timeline or two he would be able to see Jesus there.

Returning to the memory scene for the second time, Tresor was tense and obviously uncomfortable. "My stomach hurts just like it did when this happened," he said.

"Of course it does," I kindly answered. "Your brain and body have very specific memory of this experience which you are remembering. We can heal all of it through the Healing Timeline," I added. Tresor seemed dubious, but willing to follow my lead.

It is important to mention a point here, which will be stressed throughout the book. Counselors must guide and maintain the process for the Healing Timeline. The client, who is activating neurons that hold painful memories, needs to rely on the calm and confidence of the counselor to guide them through many repetitions of the timeline. I knew that Tresor's trauma could be resolved due to the integration process. Tresor did not have this confidence in the beginning of our work because he had not experienced the HTL before and he was briefly feeling some of the symptoms from the trauma as he remembered it. Activating some symptoms from the trauma is very temporary and can be resolved within a few timelines. The counselor's encouragement is important for helping clients continue in the HTL process when it gets a bit uncomfortable for them.

I asked again if Tresor could see Jesus in the memory scene as he was remembering it for the second time.

"No," he replied again.

"That's fine," I reassured him.

"This trauma from the war is over," I repeated and we began the timeline again. I said, "Remember when your dad came home from work in the middle of the day and reported that the rebels were in the village."

Tresor nodded.

"Hiding under the sheets with a stomach ache."

Tresor nodded again.

"Evening came with brief moments of quiet and you feared the dog would bark and the rebels would burst through the door."

"Yes," he answered.

"At night you occasionally fell asleep with your head under the sheets. Each time you awakened your stomach hurt."

"Yes."

"In the morning it was quiet, but the shooting began again before noon."

We proceeded through five more cues for that day and five cues for the next day. Using a cue for each of the following few days, we completed the timeline up to his present age.

When we returned to the memory scene for the third time, Tresor said he could imagine Jesus in the memory scene. "He's watching over me. He loves me," Tresor reported. "He didn't mean for me to be a victim. There's a lot he wants me to do." I guided him through a timeline using all the cues from the two traumatic days, plus several cues for the next week and months.

Imagining the memory scene for the fourth time, Tresor said, "Jesus is there. He is sitting on my bed now. He's looking at me. It's going to be all right. He's smiling. He wants me to go play with my sister."

"It's really different knowing how it turns out, isn't it?" I asked.

With a huge exhale, he answered, "It really is. It is really helpful to know how it turned out. The 15 year-old never knew this!" Tresor exclaimed with excitement and relief. His shoulders softened and his stomach released. I guided him through another timeline.

At the end of the timeline, I asked the adult Tresor how he was doing now.

"I feel very good," he answered, smiling in disbelief. "I can't remember when I felt like this," he said with amazement.

"Does your stomach hurt?"

"No, not at all."

In the memory scene for the fifth time, Tresor reported that he could see Jesus there. "Jesus is sitting by the 15-year-old and holding his hand. He needs to know he's going to make it through this. He didn't know that he would make it."

"Let's show him the timeline," I coached and read all the memory cues again. At the end of the timeline, Tresor offered, "He didn't do very well at school the year after that. He is surprised he made it to college. He has always wanted to go to college."

Back in the memory scene again, Tresor said, "Jesus is there and he is always going to be there for him. He is not alone."

"How is the fifteen-year-old doing now?"

"He's really happy about college. He's sure now that he is going to make it through the trauma of the rebels coming to our village. What amazes him most is that there was still life after that day." We proceeded through another timeline.

Tresor remembered the memory scene followed by timelines approximately twenty times. After ten timelines, the fifteen-year-old was no longer distressed, but important thoughts or comments kept coming from Jesus so I continued to guide him to the memory scene. Plus, the fifteen-year-old did not want to stop looking at the images in the timelines!

Our complete Healing Timeline session took approximately ninety minutes. In those ninety minutes, Tresor went from feeling the actual fear and body sensations of his terrified fifteen year-old-self to an ecstatic twenty-six-year old who couldn't believe healing like this was possible. When asked how he was doing in the present, Tresor replied in amazement, "I feel very good. I don't remember feeling like this before." His smile was remarkable and we both felt awe at God's presence and healing work. "One of the things I love," Tresor said, "is hearing God like that. I've never heard God talk to me before."

At the end of our session, Tresor was exhilarated from the healing. I told him that he would probably be tired after our session and he might have unusual dreams. Within the half hour, he remarked, "Yes, I am getting very tired," and he reported that his head felt the typical fuzzy, or 'stirred' feeling that often accompanies the Healing Timeline.

The next morning he reported having slept very deeply, but he still felt a little disoriented. "I still feel very good," he exuberantly added. The second day after our session, Tresor offered with a smile, "Even my breathing has changed. It is becoming more relaxed. I have been praying that God would heal me before I graduate from college. I graduate in three months and he has answered my prayers."

After Tresor returned to college he sent this email, "A peace that I have never experienced is in my heart. I don't even remember having felt like this.

"I feel a lot of transformation in my life since the conference last Friday. I have felt a lot more confident and secure in every challenge I have had during the week. I also feel more confident in the work I want to do in Congo. For a long time, I knew what God wanted me to do, but I was afraid to take the steps. I am praying about starting an organization stateside for the work I am doing in Congo. An important relationship has been a lot better and I have been told I seem less insecure. I am really thankful to the Lord for that."

The Healing Timeline work continued to affect Tresor's life. Several months after his session, the positive outcomes he experienced at the conference were still in place and growing. Generally, the HTL produces benefits for weeks after a session. Tresor continued to respond to situations in new ways and noticed increasing insight about himself. This emerging self-awareness is typical from the Healing Timeline. Tresor saw other ways in which the war had affected him. These, too, could become targets for other HTL sessions.

Biafran War

Phil, a professional man in the United States, grew up in the civil war of Nigeria, Africa.

I worked with Phil for three sessions using the Healing Timeline. He had other primary issues that needed to be addressed but these could not be healed until his memories from the war were resolved.

An experienced marriage therapist referred Phil to me because he and his wife Mary were not being successful in their marriage counseling. The marriage therapist had worked with them for several weeks but the three of them agreed they were not making very good progress. After six sessions, the counselor suggested Phil and Mary pursue individual counseling instead of couple's therapy. Mary had trauma from her childhood and Phil had never done any healing work regarding his time as a child in the war.

From ages seven to eleven Phil lived in the midst of the Biafran War, a civil war in Nigeria from 1966 to 1970.

When a reference came up in couple's counseling regarding Phil's childhood, he broke into tears and could not finish his statements. The counselor surmised each of them needed to resolve difficulties from their childhoods in order to build their relationship together. They were referred to separate counselors.

Phil began our first session by trying to explain why he had to come to my office for therapy. His presenting issue was about the war, but he was barely able to speak about it at the intake session. Seeing his pain in referencing the war, I joined him in avoiding the war topic. Instead he gave me background information about himself. His father worked for a British company with holdings in Nigeria. Phil's father moved the family from London to western Nigeria where Phil was born. He was raised in rural Nigeria and developed deep friendships with his Nigerian peers. Together they attended a small local school where one teacher taught many grades. After school they played soccer and freely roamed among the villages. Phil described this part of his life as a childhood of freedom and peace with wonderful friendships.

In 1966, when Phil was seven, a group of military officers overthrew the central and regional governments of Nigeria. They killed the prime ministers of the Northern and Western regions. Riots followed in the north and thousands of Nigerians were killed as an aftermath of the riots. In 1967, the Eastern part of Nigeria declared itself an independent republic called Biafra. Civil war followed between Biafra and the rest of Nigeria. An estimated three million people died in the Biafran war from disease, starvation, and killings. Biafra surrendered in January 1970.

In his boyhood region, Phil was closely impacted by the war. Although he was personally not a target for killing, on more than one occasion he was present in a village or area where mass killings occurred. Nicknamed "White Boy," he could safely enter the villages of his school friends. It was not uncommon for him to personally beg tribal leaders to spare the lives of people he knew. If he learned of someone's father who was in danger of being killed, Phil ran to tribal leaders to plead for the life of a family friend. "Sometimes I was successful," he said. "Other times I was not." At a very young age Phil charged himself with the responsibility to save as many people as he could.

As a grown man, Phil said he had never once in his lifetime been able to talk about the Biafran war. His crying kept him from telling the story any time he began to say something about it. When he briefly mentioned the war in our intake session, he became too emotional to continue. Even though it was the reason he came for counseling, I assured Phil he didn't need to tell me the details of his story in order for us to heal the experience. Instead, I gave him the homework assignment of creating a timeline of his life, from age two to the present, with neutral memories if possible. I reassured him healing would not be accomplished by telling the story. I was confident the Healing Timeline would produce the emotional changes Phil was seeking and it did not require him to share very much about this subject which was so painful to him. I correctly guessed he would be able to share his story after the Healing Timeline.

Phil brought his completed timeline to our second session. It had one memory for each year of his life, such as "age six: playing soccer with Nigerian friends; age seven: riding in my father's Land Rover; age eight: the cook making bread." I did not want to begin the Healing Timeline without Phil's written cues because I suspected he would be very emotional when we began to focus on the war, and I wanted to move him steadily through repetitions of the timeline. We prayed together at the beginning of our session.

To begin our counseling, I asked Phil to close his eyes and ask Jesus to take him to the right memory to begin healing his memories from the war. After a few moments Phil said, "I can see myself at eight years old trying to save people from death." He could barely express the image in his mind due to his tears.

"What are you seeing?" I asked.

"I see myself in front of the Headman of a village. My father has gone away on a patrol and I thought it was my job as an eight-year-old to be like my father. I patrolled our community. That's why I was in these villages. I'm standing in front of the Headman begging for him to spare a life." Phil started crying heavily.

"Can you imagine Jesus being in the memory with you?" I asked.

"I can see him there," Phil eventually answered. "With Jesus standing there I understand I didn't have any responsibility to patrol or attempt to save people's lives. I was a child. I completely put this on myself." Phil turned away, crying.

"It's over," I gently answered. "Remember age nine when the cook was baking bread."

Phil continued to quietly sob. "It really is over," I quietly repeated. "Remember when the cook was baking bread...."

Through his tears, Phil acknowledged the memory. Then I read the cue for age ten, "Remember your father going on patrols while you stayed home frightened with your mother."

Again, he nodded through tears.

I continued through his written timeline until we reached his current age of fifty-four. At the end of the timeline we were silent together. Phil was deeply pensive and I waited. He shook his head in disbelief. "I was a child," he said again, mournfully. "I put that responsibility on myself to be like my father. I wanted to please him so badly."

Gently, I nudged, "Can you see yourself in front of the Headman again?"

Drawn out of his reflection, he sighed and said, "Yes, I can see myself there. I've never thought about why I tried to save the people. I did it to please my dad. I wanted him to notice me. I thought he was very brave to make patrols and I was imitating him."

"What's happening in the image with the Headman? Can you see Jesus there?"

"Yes, I can see him there. Jesus is not really saying anything, but seeing this memory with Jesus present I understand on a deep level I was only a child and it was not my responsibility to save people from the war. I completely put this on myself. I have never thought of this before," Phil strongly emphasized, amazed at his new revelation. He tried to speak again but was choked by his tears.

"It's over," I compassionately said again.

Phil was absorbed in his new awareness. Rather than let him linger too long in the memory, I coached him again that it was over. "Remember age nine when the cook was baking bread." Phil nodded. "And age ten, your dad was going on patrols." Phil nodded again and we completed another timeline.

At the end of the second timeline we took a break and discussed Phil's new insight. He was able to talk about the significant new understanding he had gained from being back in the memory of pleading for lives in front of the Headman. With Jesus present in the memory he had grasped on a deep, spirit-level the truth that he was only a

child then and did not really have any power or responsibility during the war. This insight had not occurred to him in
any of his nearly five decades since the war. It was only by
revisiting the memory and experiencing Jesus' perspective
in the scene that Phil understood the profound truth he was
merely a child in a bad situation and that he, himself, had
erroneously assumed adult responsibility.

During the break, Phil talked about his relationship
with his father. He longed for the attention of his dad, whom
he described as 'hard and preoccupied.' Phil said, "My
father made it very clear to me the way to win his love was
through accomplishing great things. At one time he said to
me, 'Our family reputation is resting on you. You're the one
who can turn things around.' He was referring to the family
heritage from England. He placed a heavy burden on me
that I worked very hard to fulfill."

"I don't think it's God's plan for a child to save the
lineage of his family," I said.

"I lived with this expectation my entire life. I tried
to get my dad's approval for as long as he lived," Phil
responded. With sadness, he was gaining greater insight
into the motivation behind his childhood behavior and its
implications throughout his lifetime.

Phil and I could have had an ongoing conversation
about his relationship to his father. Instead, I guided Phil
to see himself in the memory scene with Jesus again. These
are the choice points counselors must make when using the

Healing Timeline. Our conversation about his father's influence would probably have been very helpful to Phil. Yet the healing through timelines would be even more powerful.

I asked Phil to return to the image of himself with the Headman again.

"I can see myself there," he said.

"What's happening now?"

"I'm standing in front of the Headman and he is proud of me."

"Can you bring Jesus in?" I asked. Phil nodded he could see Jesus in the image. "What is he saying or doing?"

"He's telling me 'They are my people and they are not forgotten.'" Phil began crying heavily again.

I reinforced Jesus' words and said, "They are his people. He has not forgotten them. Jesus is responsible for them, not you." Phil nodded in acknowledgement. I waited quietly again while Phil reflected on the words and compassion of Jesus, seeing himself as a child in Jesus' presence.

After a few minutes, with increased understanding, he gently said, "There are people lying in pits. I want to give them an identity. I want to tell their story." Phil's words seemed much more adult-like, a healthy response to a tragic occurrence.

"Let's finish with another timeline," I proposed. "Remember age nine when the cook was baking bread."

Familiar with our sequencing, Phil nodded and we progressed through a third timeline.

At the end of the timeline, Phil quickly opened his eyes and said from a very adult perspective, "I really do want to write a book about Biafra's genocide. I'm going to call it *White Boy in Africa*. I'm going to write it as a tribute to the millions of people who died." Remarkably, Phil was very composed as he clearly projected the concept of a book teaching about the genocide. "People don't really know what happened," he said. "I'm going to write a book about it." It was noticeable that no tears accompanied Phil's discussion about writing his experiences from Nigeria specifically focusing on the Biafran war. I gave him encouragement to write the book at the right time.

"I'm going to write it," he confirmed again from a very self-assured, confident position.

"I hope you do," I answered truthfully.

We concluded our first timeline session regarding the war. Wisely, and without my influence, the session had focused on responsibility. The Holy Spirit showed us it was the first important step in releasing Phil from the trauma he had experienced as a child. By the end of the first timeline session Phil was able to understand he was a child in the war who did not have personal responsibility for saving lives. He understood he had put that burden on himself as a way to gain his father's love and approval. Jesus made it clear to the eight-year-old Phil that he, Jesus, was responsible for the people of Nigeria and he had not forgotten them. Not surprisingly, an adult action step emerged after Phil understood he did not carry personal responsibility for the war but could contribute something positive now in the aftermath of a tragic situation.

A week later we focused on the war again. After our customary prayers for Jesus' healing, Phil said he was being led back to a childhood memory. He began to cry and said, "I don't know if I can tell you this. It's really terrible." He turned away, saying, "I need a minute to deal with this." I waited quietly, wanting to respect his internal process but watching to make sure he didn't become too overwhelmed with emotion. He turned away to focus on the replay movie in his mind and shook his head back and forth silently. "I don't have the confidence to do what I have to do," he murmured, seeing the images in his mind.

Opening his eyes and turning to me he said, "I was incredibly young...a very, very innocent, blonde-haired kid...small, too."

I affirmed he was right and asked, "What are you seeing?"

With eyes closed he said, "It's really terrible," as a warning for me to prepare for what I might hear and also as an observation about the image in his mind.

"I'm sure it is," I validated. "You don't have to tell me but we can still heal it."

"It's pure bloody mayhem. Bloody killing is happening around me as I'm hiding in a cornfield furrow with my Nigerian friends. One soldier finds us lying there and waves his sword aggressively over us, teasing us with our lives."

"Would you bring Jesus in?" I asked.

Phil remained silent, shaking his head back and forth, drawn into the memory on the screen of his mind.

"Is Jesus there?" I interrupted

Prompted out of his inner reflection, Phil said, "Yes, I can see him there. He's very angry about what is happening. He is overlooking the field of war where the bloody madness is occurring. I can see him coming to me personally. He comes and lifts me out of the dirt where I'm lying. He takes me to a safe place."

"We're going to show that little boy he's not in the war anymore," I said. "Remember age nine when the cook was baking bread."

Phil had difficulty following the cues through the timeline. Repeatedly, I mentioned the same cue two or three times before he could disconnect his mind from the war enough to remember the event I was suggesting. With difficulty we made our way through the first timeline. At the end of it he said, "I was really little...and young."

I compassionately agreed.

Without a break, I asked Phil to envision himself in the furrow again while the war spread around him.

"I'm there with my little friends. It's pure, bloody

mayhem. I'm frozen in time—frozen out there with my boys."

"Can you bring Jesus in?" I asked.

"Yes, he's there. He's taking me out of the furrow again to a safe place. I feel my body relaxing as he takes me out of there. In the safe place I see his sadness. He's crying about what is happening. He's very sad."

"Can you imagine him assuring you that you're safe now?"

"Yes, I can. I can imagine Jesus saying that to me because it's true. I am safe now."

"Let's show the little boy the timeline again," I suggested. "Can you think of your own memory for age nine or would you like me to read the cues?" I asked.

"I think I can do it on my own," Phil agreed, so I mentioned age nine and waited until he got a spontaneous memory, then moved onto the rest of his ages up to age fifty-four.

After a total of four timelines Phil was very calm. He said, "Right now, when I think about the war, I feel neutral. I don't even feel the sadness. Right before the last timeline, in the safe place with Jesus, I was looking across the grasslands and wondering what I would do for the world. I could see things. The little boy is a visionary."

Once again, after the trauma-related emotions were released, Phil naturally moved into constructive ways of thinking. He reconnected with himself as a visionary, a young person who would make a contribution to the world. This dramatic shift from overwhelming negative feelings to a positive view is a common outcome from each session of the Healing Timeline.

Before we concluded our session, Phil said, "My company is sending me to Nigeria in a couple of months. I will be within an hour's plane ride of the region where I grew up. I think I'll pay my own way and fly up there while I'm in the country. I'd like to see it again." Phil's mood had significantly shifted from the intake session in which he could not mention the war without crying. I marveled at the amazing work of the Holy Spirit. Phil had not returned to Nigeria during his adulthood and yet we were healing his trauma a few months before he was scheduled to fly there for business. As usual, I was awed by God's timing and power.

Phil began our fourth session with an interesting report. Two times during the week he was able to discuss his experiences in the Biafran war with colleagues. He could not believe the difference. "I have never, in five decades, been able to discuss the war without crying," he said. "As soon as I get the first words out I choke up and then can't say anymore. Over lunch last week I talked about my experiences in the war with a colleague. We bantered back and forth over lunch and I was able to talk about it easily. That has never, and I mean never, happened in my life before. What have you done to me?" he joked. "How could that happen in two sessions?" he asked incredulously.

"Well, you're really smart," I replied, "and that's how this works. Once your child-brain understands the war is over you can carry on like an adult. Talking about it with a trusted friend was an adult thing to do. Writing your book about it is also an adult thing to do. You're not done, though," I added.

"I know," he said. "I can tell there's more work to do, but I can't believe what's happened already. A team from Nigeria came to my work last week and I was able to talk with them about living in the country. Before, when other teams have come, I have withdrawn and not mentioned that I was raised in Nigeria, too. And another thing," he added exuberantly, "I'm doing better at work. I've made two presentations at work this week and I'm so calm I can't believe it's me. I made my presentations to the Board of Directors, which would have intimidated me before, but this week I just organized my notes before the lecture, presented the material, and left knowing I had done a good job. Usually I'm overcome with anxiety wanting their approval. I know they are the company Board of Directors, but this week I just gave them what they needed to hear from me, and then went back to my office and attended to other work I needed to do. I didn't worry or fret about what they thought about me. How do you do it?" he asked again.

"Your brain does the work," I repeated. "I just set you up to change your brain."

"Yeah, yeah," he said, laughing. "I've been to counseling before and nothing like this has ever happened to me. You're doing something different," he insisted.

"You're right," I acknowledged. "The Healing Timeline is really different and really powerful. And you are doing a really good job with it. How are you feeling this week about the war?"

"I feel better. I'm staying on my medication, but I definitely feel better."

I admonished Phil to stay on his medication until his prescribing physician directed him otherwise. We prayed, asking God to direct our session, and Phil gave God permission to go anywhere in his conscious or subconscious mind for healing. After a few quiet moments, Phil said, "I see myself as a little boy on the veranda with my mom. We had a big porch that looked out over the grasslands and I'm sitting there with her. My dad has gone off to his patrols and we're both scared, very scared."

"Can you bring Jesus in?"

"Yes, I can see him with us. He's talking with us, saying things are going to turn out fine. He knows how scared we are. He reassures us my dad will live." Phil turned to me, opening his eyes and said, "He does live. It's helpful to know the end of the story, isn't it?"

"Yes," I assured him. "Jesus knows everything and he knew your dad would make it through the war."

"There were lots of scary things about the war. As we're sitting on the veranda together I can see how much my mother worried about losing my father on his patrols. Our home was safe, but I guess we never knew for sure if my dad would come back."

"What is Jesus doing or saying?"

"He's reassuring us we all live through the war and he is with us. Jesus will be there with us on the veranda while we wait for my dad. My mom is reading to me and Jesus is sitting peacefully on the steps listening."

"Let's show the little boy his whole family made it through the war and all this is over," I said. We proceeded through the timeline, which went very smoothly. I began by giving Phil the written cue from his timeline sheet and he quickly acknowledged each memory that came to mind.

When we returned to the memory scene on the veranda, Phil said he felt much safer after the first timeline. I asked him to bring Jesus in again, which he was able to do. During our three timeline sequences, Jesus joined Phil and his mother on the porch, reassuring him of their safety and Jesus' own presence with them. In the third visit to the memory scene Phil imagined the little boy playing in the yard, knowing his dad lived through the war and they all stayed safe.

At the end of the third timeline Phil was very peaceful. He said, "I have unfinished business about the war. A calling has been given to me. Those who died should not be forgotten. This is a circle with a missing piece. I make up the missing piece. I have to write the book in memory of the people who died in the war. There are other genocides in the world. People need to learn from genocides."

I reflected again on God's amazing timing: Phil was being healed of the memories and emotions he had carried throughout his lifetime regarding the war, he emerged from the Healing Timeline sessions with a desire to write about his experiences, and his company was sending him near Nigeria within a few months. Wow. God is amazing.

Phil and I went on to target other issues in his life. He started therapy because he was struggling in his marriage and he very much wanted to address some relationship aspects of his life. Since Phil's distress about the war continued to remain low, I agreed to work with him on other targets. He continued to be able to talk about the war without crying and was generally at peace about his experiences there. I sensed it would be helpful to address more aspects of the war with Phil, but relationship issues felt more pressing to him. We may return to the war at another time, but for now Phil is grateful, amazed, and growing dramatically through the work of the Healing Timeline.

Phil's story is a good example of unexpected changes occurring for the client through the Healing Timeline. Even though we were targeting the Biafran war and he was experiencing tremendous relief from his post-traumatic stress disorder, by the third week of counseling his work life was going much better. He said he was calm at work and was able to make presentations without the strong approval-seeking anxiety he usually experienced. During our first timeline session, Phil understood the connection between his approval-seeking behavior and his childhood motivation for going on self-appointed patrols as an eight-year-old boy. As a child, he was desperate for the love of his father and thought he could earn his father's approval by imitating him in the war. When Phil's dad went on patrols, so did little Phil. As Phil released his childhood way of thinking, his adult work behavior changed. He no longer saw each presentation before the Board of Directors as an opportunity for approval in absentia. Instead, he made his presentations and went back to work. He said, "It's even easier for me to organize my thoughts now. I know what I want to say and I say it." His reduced anxiety about approval made it easier for him to accomplish his work.

Phil's case evidenced another common outcome of the Healing Timeline. He began to have increasing insight about himself and his own contributions to the relationship difficulties he was having. Phil, like all of us, carried his child-self into current-day relationships and his child-self was victimized. Children are powerless to solve grown-up problems like wars. As a young boy caught in a war, he actually was a victim. It is not surprising he felt victimized in his adult relationships. Even though we only focused on the war in the beginning of our work, Phil began to see relationship issues in his life from a much more realistic perspective. He was able to think in broader, more adult ways, rather than believe he was a victim in his relationships. When he began to heal his childhood trauma from the war, Phil was able to see he was a contributor to the marital problems, not just a victim of them.

Phil had other pressing emotional issues which needed to be addressed to improve his marriage and work life. We went on to specifically work with his relationship problems and their roots. Undoubtedly, it would be helpful to continue focusing on aspects of the war at some time in the future. Yet the three sessions he experienced with the Healing Timeline brought great relief to Phil and enabled him to focus his attention on healing the marriage.

Four months after we targeted Phil's experience in the Biafran war, he traveled to South Africa for business. Although he was within an hour's flight from his boyhood home, he was not able to return to the region due to military tensions. Yet he saw evidence of current, ongoing violence in the parts of South Africa where he was visiting. Machine guns and security officers were stationed on second-story lookouts at his hotel. Phil had to proceed through security scanners and live searches in order to enter the building. After the work assignment, he traveled within the region and was told of the murders and vandalism that were still occurring in South Africa.

These stories and the machine guns perched over his hotel did not in any way trigger earlier trauma from the Biafran War. He said, "I saw a lot of guns and it did not

activate my PTSD." He went on to tell of his experience visiting a church where children had been slaughtered in the
genocide. Bullet holes remained in the sanctuary as ongoing reminders of apartheid and mass killings. Although he
was saddened by apartheid, Phil did not become emotional,
anxious, or overwhelmed by his own childhood experience
of civil war. The three sessions using the Healing Timeline
had resolved his post-traumatic stress disorder and no trace
of it appeared during his visit to the continent where it
occurred.

Reflecting on our work together, Phil said, "Into my
fifties, I struggled with the effects of having been a child in
a genocide war in Africa. The integration from the timeline
process changed my life. I am healed in so many ways I give
thanks everyday."

Six

Sexual Abuse and Promiscuity

Sexual abuse for men and women is one of the most common issues clients bring to counseling. It comprises fifty percent of the presenting issues for which individuals seek out pastoral and prayer counseling in their churches. It is not a pleasant subject to discuss, but we need to address the concerns of those who have been affected by sexual abuse. Sexual abuse victims want healing but are often not sure how to get the healing they need. Sometimes they are not able to seek out counseling because talking about the trauma is too painful or they don't remember the abuse. They might suspect something happened in their childhoods, but their memories are vague and they are afraid to delve too deeply for fear of what they might find. The Healing Timeline is an ideal modality for treating sexual abuse.

When sexual abuse happens, emotional and psychological damage is inflicted in several ways. When using the HTL to address issues of sexual abuse it is necessary to address the common feelings which are present in the story of virtually every sexual abuse survivor: confusion, powerlessness, and shame. We all have an organic, appropriate sense of what is right and safe in our lives and the sexual approach of an abuser violates our inherent self-knowing. Victims feel confused about what is happening to them especially if they are children.

Sexual abuse victims feel powerless. Due to their age or circumstance, victims feel the powerlessness of not being able to avert a serious problem they did not want and did not create. There can be multiple consequences for resisting or yielding to a perpetrator's approach. This places abuse victims in a double-bind situation they are powerless to resolve. One predator told a two-year-old, "I will throw you out the second-story window if you tell anyone." Perpetrators threaten victims with lies about the well-being of others whom they love if the victim does not give them what they want. Many victims believed these lies and hold themselves responsible for their sexual abuse. Through the HTL sequences they need to be validated that they were powerless victims who did the best they could. They are not guilty for the sexual abuse even if they were told a lie to make them believe otherwise.

Perpetrators have twisted thinking, which they visit on their victims. One man told a 13-year-old, "I knew you wanted me when I saw you in that blue dress." This is a manipulative lie that confused and blamed an adolescent for the perpetrator's behavior. As counselor and client move through the layers of sexual trauma, victims need to be reassured they were powerless in their abusive situations no matter what they were told.

Shame is present for most sexual abuse victims. Their mistreatment violates the internal sense of self. Confusion, powerlessness, and the violence of sexual abuse cause victims to internalize an erroneous belief there is something profoundly wrong with them. Children, who are appropriately open to the love of trusted adults, obviously feel badly when they are violated. They do not have complex enough thinking to separate how they feel from who they are. Being treated badly leads to feeling bad inside and is internalized as "I am bad." This form of thinking becomes stored in the brain. Healing begins when clients are led to change their beliefs in the "ring" or section of their lives where false beliefs were stored. The Healing Timeline process will likely uncover feelings of shame when the trauma is re-visited. Addressing the shame and replacing lies about the self are very important steps in working with sexual abuse victims.

Jamie's story is typical of sexual abuse, as is the healing which occurred for her through the Healing Timeline. Even though abuse may be difficult to talk about, every client who has experienced the Healing Timeline has later been able to speak of it in neutral, non-emotionally charged terms. The healthy steps they take for restoration after the healing are impressive and not forced. Removing the emotion from the trauma aids them in addressing the problems of the trauma. When healing sexual abuse through the HTL, clients always change their internal belief system, which results in changed behaviors. Jamie, age 39, fits this profile.

Jamie grew up in a Christian home in an active church family. Her father was a leader in their local church. Unfortunately, Jamie's father repeatedly abused her sexually when she was a child. By age sixteen Jamie was sexually active. It is common for children who have been sexually abused when young to seek out sexual relationships in their adolescence. Because their sexual barriers were violated in childhood by someone they loved, adolescents often choose to be promiscuous in their teen years and beyond. When their own sexuality blossoms, teens are already acquainted with sexualized relationships. Jamie began to have sex with her peers by age fourteen and was pregnant at age sixteen. She came to prayer counseling very provocatively dressed.

Jamie was encouraged by a family member to seek out healing prayer in a nearby church. She was not a regular church-attender, but her brother had experienced the Healing Timeline with great benefit. He encouraged her to try the Healing Timeline for her own life. In the first session Jamie appeared very sullen and discouraged. Her presenting issue was very clear. She had been divorced three times and was currently living with a married man. Her goal for therapy was to have the relationship with her married, live-in partner work out successfully.

Susan, the prayer counselor, replied to her goal, "I'm sorry, I can't pray for that, but we can pray about life in general." She continued by saying, "Maybe some of the things that got you to the point of making destructive choices could be healed."

Jamie was open to talking about the possibility of general healing. Susan guided them in a prayer asking God to only allow his truth to be spoken in their session and the lies of the enemy to be silenced. Susan has found that saying these prayers in the beginning of prayer counseling shifts the direction of the session. Clients are amazed where God leads them when the prayer room is cleansed of all enemy forces and only truth is allowed to be spoken and heard in their time together.

Susan sensed Jamie's anxiety and said, "You can relax because we're only here to love you and Jesus is going to do the rest." Jamie gave God permission to go anywhere he desired in her consciousness or unconsciousness and he led her to a memory at age fourteen.

Jamie described herself as a tomboy who was never pretty like her sisters. She found that junior high school boys would pay attention to her if she agreed to have sex with them. Being hungry for attention, she began to have regular sexual relationships with the boys from school. One evening when she was coming home late, her mother found out she had been with a boy and raged at her, calling her vile names. Jamie's first prayer counseling session went back to the memory of that night.

In describing the scene, Jamie said, "I believed I was ugly and I needed to make these compromises to be loved. I didn't feel loved in any other part of my life." Susan coached her to invite Jesus into the memory.

As soon as she could see Jesus in the memory scene Jamie began to cry. "He's telling me he loves me and I don't have to do anything to deserve his love." Because Jamie was very emotional hearing this truth, Susan guided her through their first timeline rather than continue in the memory scene. The memories were mostly negative ones on the first repetition of the timeline.

When they returned to the memory scene, Jamie was still quite emotional. In the image she could hear Jesus explaining to her she didn't need to seek out sex with teenage boys to feel loved. She described him as speaking the truth to her without condemnation. Jamie said, "When I was fourteen I didn't know I had any other ways for getting love. I felt really terrible about myself and this seemed like the only way to get attention." Susan guided her through another timeline, which also contained mostly negative memories.

On the third time returning to the memory scene, Jesus intervened with Jamie's mother who was struggling in her marriage. Jesus spoke to her with compassion, saying, "What you are telling your daughter is not true." Jesus went on to tell Jamie the truth, replacing every lie with a positive word, concluding with, "You are my beloved." Jamie was deeply touched by Jesus speaking so tenderly to her and standing up for her. Susan led Jamie through a third timeline, which included spontaneous memories of her successes and memories of people saying kind things to her. Overall, it was significantly more positive than the first two timelines.

They returned to the memory scene a fourth time and listened again to Jesus' intervention. Jesus explained to Jamie that she was a very smart, talented young woman whom he desired to raise up into her gifts. He said, "I have something important I want you to do for me." Jamie had never felt important in her life, and she imagined herself falling asleep in the memory scene with his kind, loving words in her ears instead of the harsh criticism from her mother. Susan led her through the fourth and final timeline, comprised of primarily positive memories. It is typical for the memories to transition from negative to positive throughout the timeline repetitions.

They closed the session by Jamie forgiving her mother for the cruel words she had spoken. In their prayer time, Jamie had grown in understanding her mother's own unhappiness and the difficult situation she was in with her father. Susan also led Jamie in prayers of breaking soul ties created between Jamie and the boys with whom she had participated in sex. Jamie was tired but relieved at the end of their session. Jesus' positive words of truth were beginning to settle into the place where Jamie's identity had been formed by her mother's hurtful words. Jamie grew up feeling worthless and only good for sex, an identity she played out as soon as she reached adolescence. Susan sensed that Jesus' truth about Jamie's core identity was beginning to replace the lies she had believed.

Two weeks later, Jamie returned for their second prayer session together. She still looked very drawn and depressed and wore the provocative clothing that was normal for her. She had experienced some positive changes over the two weeks between sessions, and her confidence was growing that this form of counseling would help her. She presented a very specific request for the focus of their time together.

Jamie became pregnant at age sixteen and gave her baby up for adoption. Crying, she told Susan the story. "I think about my baby almost every day and I can't get past it. Even though it was almost twenty years ago, I'm haunted by the story. Nothing I've done in counseling has helped me let go of my mistake. I feel so badly about what I did. I have no idea where my baby is now." Susan assured her Jesus would heal her with his truth and they began their session focused on this topic.

After the usual prayers, Susan asked Jamie to invite

Jesus to guide them to the right place for healing. After a few quiet moments, Jamie said, "I'm remembering the delivery room when my daughter was born. My mom and dad were there. It should have been a happy time, but it was mixed up with shame and sorrow. They didn't even let me hold my baby. They said it was best for me to let her go before I could get attached."

"Can you invite Jesus into the memory?" Susan asked. Jamie was crying so hard she was not able to answer. Looking for a nod, Susan repeated, "Is Jesus there?"

Jamie was still not able to reply. Susan said, "Being the sixteen-year-old girl in the delivery room is over," and she guided Jamie through a timeline.

When they returned to the image in the delivery room Jamie said through tears, "I don't even know my little girl but I love her. I want to see my baby. I messed up my life and hers. My parents aren't supportive of me at all." Susan guided her to invite Jesus into the memory again.

"Is he there?" she asked.

"I don't know," Jamie mumbled, crying.

"Well that time is over," Susan said kindly, and led Jamie through another timeline. Emotion decreases steadily through repetitions of the timeline and Susan knew they would eventually be able to see and hear Jesus in the memory scene.

Returning to the memory scene for the third time, Jamie offered, "I can see Jesus holding my baby. He looks right into my eyes and says, 'Everything is going to be all right.' He's going to look after my baby. He can be with her when I cannot be there for her. He's telling me she is going to a really good family who is praying for a baby. He has a perfect plan, which is going to work out. It makes me feel a lot better hearing Jesus say this to me. I've tried to tell myself before that Jesus was looking after her, but I guess I never really believed it." Susan guided her through a third timeline. At the end of the timeline, Jamie was still very sad but able to think differently about her baby's birth. She said, "This is the hardest thing that has ever happened in my life. Maybe now I can get over it." Susan replied affirmatively, promising her Jesus can heal everything.

Together they revisited the birth scene three more times, following each visit with the timeline. Jesus promised Jamie that her baby would have a very different life than the one she had lived. Jamie was comforted by his reassurance regarding her baby. Unlike her parents, Jesus communicated how happy he was about the baby's birth. He also spoke positive truth to her about her identity and value to him. Again she heard Jesus' words of love for her and his plan to use her in wonderful ways. Before these two prayer counseling sessions, Jamie had assumed someone like her was not a valuable person to Jesus and his kingdom. Not only was she receiving emotional healing about her most difficult memories, she was beginning to internalize the truth Jesus had a plan for her and she had not disqualified herself from being in his love.

At the end of the session Jamie said, "I didn't think I would ever get over this but I can see now it was a long time ago. I was just a kid when I had a baby. After hearing Jesus' words to me I can trust my baby is in good hands. I've always wanted to register with a service in case she wanted to find me. Before today I have thought, *she'll never want to find someone like me,* but now I think I can register. After all, I'm the one who loved her first." Her tone and demeanor were very different than they were in the beginning of the session.

From that session forward, Jamie reported she was able to talk about her baby's adoption and birth experience without tears. Each time she saw Susan, she hugged her and said, "It's unbelievable how differently I feel about my baby's birth. I didn't think this was possible. Thank you!" Jamie's brother attended Susan's church. He sought Susan out and confirmed Jamie's confidence was growing. For the first time she was able to talk about her adopted baby with hope instead of shame and defeat.

Jamie and Susan met two more times for prayer counseling. Each time, Jamie marveled that her feelings about the adoption had been remarkably changed for the better. For the remaining two sessions Jamie's priority was still to focus on her relationship with her live-in, married partner. She was longing for their relationship to become permanent.

In each session, Susan reminded her they would seek God's truth and healing wherever he wanted to lead them and Jamie agreed. For each of those two sessions, the Holy Spirit led them to memories with various men in Jamie's life. He spoke words of truth and validation to her, and communicated that she did not need to spend her time in bad situations. Each session involved four or more timelines in which the memories began as primarily negative ones and shifted to increasingly positive memories. At the end of the fourth session, Jamie said she needed a break from counseling. She left with her goal intact of desiring to see her relationship work out with the married man with whom she was living.

A month later Jamie contacted Susan to schedule one more appointment. Jamie began the prayer session by announcing, "I've broken up with the man I was living with. His counselor told him he shouldn't see me until his divorce is final and I'm great with that. I don't think I want to see him anymore." Susan perceived that the previous Healing Timeline sessions were producing change in Jamie's life evidenced by the significant shift in her attitude and relationship toward the married man.

The next time Susan and Jamie met was in a chance encounter at a shopping mall. Jamie greeted Susan with a big hug and thanked her for being the woman who had changed her life. Jamie had begun attending church regularly and described herself as growing in the Lord. Her faith had become very important to her. She was also seeking a job change for two reasons. She was tired of doing the work she had been doing when she first began prayer counseling with Susan and it was the place where she often met men with whom she developed sexual relationships. In many ways, it was not unlike her junior high school days. She had gone to work looking for love like the junior high student who had gone to school looking for attention. After the five sessions with the Healing Timeline, Jamie understood she didn't need to have sex to feel loved nor did she want to be in an environment that made her feel inferior.

Many internal changes had taken place for Jamie and she was shifting her external world to match the changes. Jamie's remarks to Susan in the shopping mall expressed her gratitude and amazement. "God has given me a brand new life," she said. "I know he has a plan for me. I didn't think it was possible to be changed like this."

Susan confirmed the wonder of the changes. Jamie did not look at all like the provocatively dressed, sullen young woman who had come into their first session together. Susan said, "If I hadn't seen it with my own eyes, I wouldn't have believed Jamie was the same person I started working with. She had a new hairstyle, was stunning and beautiful. She looked like a different person, radiant. I couldn't get over the beauty that radiated from the inside out. God gets all the glory," she concluded.

Jamie's story typifies the process of 'God taking the ghetto out of us and us taking ourselves out of the ghetto.'

Everyone who has experienced sexual abuse can be restored. By repeatedly asking God to guide clients to the right memories, sexual abuse victims can become reconnected to the person God created them to be rather than identifying with themselves as sexualized victims. Once the healing has taken place at the point of injury, men and women will take themselves out of the situations where they had naturally gravitated due to their sexual abuse. It is a privilege and blessing to observe this process over and over for the lives of sexual abuse victims.

Seven

Life's Anxieties

Many people have fears and anxieties that might be considered irrational but are real nonetheless. These fears include anxiety about driving over bridges, being in elevators, seeing insects, driving on certain roadways, and undergoing medical procedures. Others who don't experience such fears might consider these conditions ridiculous, but to those who suffer from life's anxieties in its many forms, their fears are very real and sometimes debilitating. The Healing Timeline can offer a solution for removing many of these fears.

The Healing Timeline is not sufficient to eradicate major anxiety disorders, but it can provide relief for anxieties that are based on specific, concrete memories. For example, a prayer team member who learned about the HTL used it to address her fear of driving over bridges. Through the prayer process, she was led to a memory which occurred five years previously when she was in a near fatal car accident on a long city bridge. In the initial session, the prayer counselor coached her to re-experience the memory scene with Jesus present four times, each followed by a timeline. The next week she reported her anxiety about driving over bridges was fifty percent reduced, which gave her the freedom to follow a driving route she usually avoided. After two follow up sessions, which focused on different aspects of the accident, her bridge anxiety was virtually gone. This type of anxiety was based on an actual event and resolved after the triggering memory was integrated through the timeline. Not all anxiety is based on specific incidences and therefore not all anxiety can be healed through the HTL method. Yet many of life's seemingly irrational anxieties have concrete events at their root and can be resolved through the Healing Timeline. Richard's story is such an account from a very capable man who was derailed by a proposed medical procedure.

Medical Anxieties

Richard's wife described him as athletic and not afraid of anything; a man who can be counted on to do "manly things." While repairing the roof gutter, Richard's ladder slipped and he fell to the ground, catching himself with his left hand. Right away Richard suspected a major injury. A trip to the doctor the next morning resulted in a cast. In light of his usual bravery, Richard's wife was surprised at his ongoing anxiety about wearing a cast and his even greater anxiety about an upcoming MRI, a medical procedure which required Richard to lay perfectly still for several minutes in a large tube while x-ray-type imaging took place. The MRI was critical for assessing how well the arm was healing, but Richard was too fearful to agree to the procedure. At his wife's suggestion, a few days before going for the MRI, Richard met with a healing prayer team.

After briefly discussing the problem and Richard's feelings related to the cast and MRI, the prayer team leader asked Richard to give God permission to go anywhere in Richard's subconscious that was necessary to heal his anxiety. Richard prayed silently as did the two other members of the prayer team. Then the prayer team leader guided Richard to ask Jesus to lead them wherever he wished in order to bring healing to this area of his life. Together they waited quietly until Richard said, "I have a memory. I can see myself as a third grader, about age nine, being grabbed by a seventh-grader in the locker room. He threw me against the lockers. I was afraid. I felt badly about myself because I was thinking I shouldn't have gotten into this situation."

It is important to note here that the Holy Spirit will always take clients to the right memory for healing even if the prayer counselor cannot see the connection between the presenting issue and the memory. The prayer counselor should not second guess if this is the correct memory, but rather trust the process and proceed by inviting Jesus into the memory.

The team leader suggested to Richard that he invite Jesus into the locker room memory. Richard said, "I can see Jesus taking the older kid and sitting him in the corner of the locker room. Jesus is standing between him and me."

The team leader asked, "Can you imagine Jesus saying, 'You didn't do anything wrong. You had every right to be there?'" She waited until Richard nodded yes, he could hear Jesus saying these things in the memory scene. Then she continued, "Imagine Jesus saying, 'You aren't to blame for his poor choices. In fact it really had nothing to do with you. A big kid was taking out his frustrations on the easiest target. There is nothing wrong with you. You didn't cause it to happen. It's over now.'"

Richard again nodded he could imagine Jesus saying these words to his younger self. Then the team leader led Richard through a timeline of his life beginning at age ten, up to his current age of forty-nine.

"Let's return to the memory again," she coached. "Before we invite Jesus in, would you tell me how the little boy is feeling now?"

"He feels a little less angst but still feels guilty, like perhaps he said something that provoked this."

The prayer team leader encouraged Richard to invite Jesus into the scene again. The other prayer team members waited quietly, praying silently, and imagining the scene as Richard described it.

"I see Jesus in the scene again," Richard reported. "The seventh grade boy is gone now and Jesus is comforting me."

The team leader prompted the internal conversation by suggesting, "Imagine Jesus saying something to you like, 'Children often feel it is their fault when something bad happens, as if they caused it. But the other child is much older and was responsible for this. It was not okay. It isn't a reflection of who you are, it was the other boy making some bad choices.'"

The team waited quietly until Richard nodded this dialogue had taken place between Jesus and his nine-year-old self.

The prayer leader continued, "Can you hear Jesus saying, 'I planned and designed you even before I made the Earth. That's how special and important you are to me?'"

Richard said, "The nine-year-old is amazed. Jesus is briefly explaining about salvation and forgiveness to him. My nine-year-old self accepts Jesus' into his heart and agrees to forgive the seventh-grader." The team leader led him through another timeline to integrate this healing.

Returning to the memory scene a third time, Richard reported he could spontaneously see Jesus and his nine-year old self on the curb across the street from school. "Does he feel any distress?" the team leader asked.

"No, not sitting there with Jesus. For some reason, right now as an adult I'm thinking about the MRI and I can hear Jesus saying to me 'It's okay to be weak. You can lean on me. I am trustworthy and in control. Even if you don't have full capacity, it's okay.' You know, 'When we are weak, He is strong.'" The team leader agreed.

Richard continued, "But I remember a time when I was nine and I did have a cast. I couldn't play baseball and I felt sad and lonely."

Because there was no distress remaining in the locker room scene, the prayer team leader moved on to Richard's cast memory. If there had been any distress remaining in the locker room scene, she would have continued asking Richard to see Jesus intervene there, followed by timelines, until no distress remained in the first memory scene.

Richard remembered being the nine-year-old in the cast and invited Jesus into the scene. "He assures me this is just for a time, he will heal my arm. Jesus understands how frustrated I am because I can't do everything I would like to do. He says I'm still valuable to him even if I'm not performing—like hitting home runs. Again, he's showing me how dependable he is even with my impairments."

At the end of this dialogue, the team leader guided Richard through another timeline of his life up to his current age. When they reached his adult age of 49, she asked if the nine-year-old was still upset at all.

"Nah," he replied. "He knows he won't be in that cast forever. It really is only for a short time. I even got to play baseball again that season. He's fine." Because the nine-year-old truly did seem fine as reported by client, the team leader went on to another topic.

If the client had given an ambiguous version of "fine" when asked about the younger self, the prayer leader would have encouraged him to enter the memory scene again. It is possible to completely heal memories through prayer and the timeline, so it is important not to stop too soon. Healing occurs so quickly with the timeline clients are grateful for the amount of healing they receive with a few timelines. Because their pain is often dramatically less than when they started, clients won't suggest revisiting the memory scene once they have begun to feel relief. The prayer counselor is in the best position to decide which should be the final timeline. In Richard's case, his body language, voice tone, and words were congruent with the sense the little boy in the memory scene was fine. Congruence between the client's words and affect is important if the client is to experience complete healing.

Since no distress was present for Richard's nine-year-old self in the locker room or cast memory, the team leader asked how he currently felt about getting an MRI. Richard said he felt relaxed about it and didn't think it would upset him. Regarding the cast that had been causing him some anxiety, he said nonchalantly, "I don't like to be restricted but I've come to terms with it." His body language and voice tone were congruent with this message.

The team debriefed their experience with Richard, sharing what they had each sensed or noticed throughout the prayer. Richard commented the timelines became more positive with each repetition, which is always the case.

As always, the Holy Spirit knew exactly where to lead Richard and the prayer team for healing. They began by focusing on the fear of being in the MRI where he would have to lie very still in a large tube for up to fifteen minutes. Through prayer, the Holy Spirit led Richard to a memory of being unexpectedly pinned down by a bully when he was a young child. He was powerless to help himself in that situation and he blamed himself for causing it to happen. A root memory of being pinned down and scared was being triggered as Richard faced the MRI in his adult life. There are probably many other connections related to the presenting problem and the float-back memories. Fortunately, we don't have to discover them in order for the client to be healed.

The cast anxiety was linked, in part, to Richard's disappointment and loneliness about having a cast in childhood and being left out of the baseball team. Anxiety is usually covering a feeling the client does not want to feel. Clients are not deliberately withholding how they feel; they simply do not know what feeling underlies their anxiety. Asking the Holy Spirit for the source memory is the best way to name and heal the underlying feeling contributing to anxious situations.

A few weeks after the prayer session, Richard reported he was able to participate in the MRI with a minimal amount of distress. As for the cast, he found it annoying for the remaining two weeks, but it did not make him afraid. In a follow-up conversation, the prayer team leader asked him to think about the nine-year-old. Richard said, "Oh, he's still doing fine. The seventh-grader really did bully me and it wasn't my fault. I'm glad that's over." He thanked the prayer team leader and said, "What you did really made a difference for me. I don't think I could have gotten through the MRI without that prayer time. Thanks."

When life's anxieties are linked to concrete memories they can be healed through the HTL method. By using enough repetitions, triggering memories can be resolved, giving clients relief for many of their anxieties.

Eight

The Healing Timeline for Children

The Healing Timeline not only transforms the childish methods used by adults, it heals children directly. Children as young as four years old have been significantly helped by the Healing Timeline. When children present their traumas and hurts for healing, they can easily be shown the "bad thing that happened" is actually over. Even if they are still in difficult circumstances, it is possible to show them, at the level where they internalized a view of themselves, that what has happened to them and around them is not their fault. This truth is a surprising revelation to children. Because it is appropriate for them to be developmentally egocentric, children assume their experiences in life are based on something they have done or something inherently wrong with them. One young client believed he caused a bad thing to happen by blinking at the lights. Children see the world from their young perspective. By assuming they cause bad things to happen, they unnecessarily form negative beliefs and assumptions about themselves. These damaging false beliefs can be reversed where they began with the Healing Timeline. By inviting Jesus to re-enter a scene from a painful situation, children can experience the truth of their traumas rather than internalize the lies and self-blaming perspective they first assume.

The steps for using the Healing Timeline with children are virtually the same as the protocol for adults. Giving God permission to go anywhere he desires within is important for children as well as adults. Most children are trusting and eager to give God permission to heal them. The process may begin by going directly into a scene the child remembers and is upset about or by asking the Holy Spirit to lead the counselor and child to the right memory for healing. When Jesus enters the memory scene most children can see or sense him because they are still strong in their use of imagination.

If there is a small time frame between a child's difficult event and the present, increments of the timeline can be shortened as much as necessary. The timeline for an injury which occurred a week ago might include a memory for each day of the week up to the present. A timeline for an incident one year ago could be counted by remembering something for every month in the year. A time frame of two years could be counted by seasons, such as memories from the fall, winter, spring, and summer. The counselor should always mention several increments in the timeline for the best integration.

When Jesus is invited into the scene and observed, it is important for the counselor to monitor what children are seeing and hearing. It is most common for them to experience Jesus as compassionate and truthful, but occasionally children put the words and heart of an angry parent onto Jesus. The counselor needs to reassure them Jesus is always caring, loving, and seeking their safety. Children in bad situations may already have a sense of angels or Jesus being close to them, speaking words of love and encouragement as they lay in bed at night. When taken through the Healing Timeline, a ten-year-old child adopted at three said she remembered angels surrounding her crib in an orphanage. The blessings of the Beatitudes are always meted out to children. (Matthew 5:3-11) When children are poor in spirit, mourn, and are needy, Jesus draws near to them in the Spirit. They may not know who has comforted them, but in some way the Holy Spirit the Comforter has already reached out to needy children. When adults heal childhood wounds, it is normal for them to say, "Even as a child I knew someone very loving was with me." Children have a natural way to experience Jesus. Most often it feels natural for children to invite him into a memory scene followed by the timeline.

The benefits of using the Healing Timeline for children are obvious. By healing the negative experiences that happen to them early, children are given the opportunity to continue growing and developing without layers of defensive strategies for protection. They can continue shining their light into the world rather than withdrawing due to lies they believed about themselves from abusive situations. All abused children are victims. No child deserves mistreatment. Yet remarkably, when children are asked if they think anything negative about themselves from the abuse they experienced, every child will say, "I'm bad," as if they caused or deserved the mistreatment. Removing this erroneous belief early is a huge gift for hurting children. Rather than fragment and emotionally split off from their negative experiences and view of themselves, children who experience the Healing Timeline while young will continue to develop with more positive truths at their core. It is much better for them to grow up knowing something bad happened to them and it is over than to believe, "I'm bad," and develop a life that matches this internal belief. Two case examples follow in which the HTL was used with children.

Jennifer's Camping Trip

Jennifer, age eight, and her family loved camping and scheduled several camping trips each summer. During their August trip they included Jennifer's aunt, who joined them in the family tent when it was time for bed. The camping lantern had been extinguished and all five members of the family were snuggled into their sleeping bags when Jennifer began to cry.

"I'm afraid to go to sleep," she said. "I don't want to sleep here tonight. I want to go home," she wailed.

Her tears surprised Jennifer's parents because Jennifer generally loved their camping experiences, especially the closeness they shared in the tent at night. On the previous trips, the family said nighttime prayers in the dark and usually started laughing together before they fell asleep. On this particular night, the prayers and the reassurance of her parents could not console Jennifer. When asked what was troubling her, Jennifer replied again, "I'm scared and I want to go home. I don't want to sleep here tonight." Each parent tried to console and reassure her she was safe in the tent with the family. Jennifer's distress continued to grow until she was very anxious about going to sleep.

Jennifer's aunt, Cynthia, had been trained in the Healing Timeline and offered to help. She suggested they ask Jesus to lead them to the source of Jennifer's distress. Jennifer agreed and said the prayer asking Jesus to take her to the right memory for healing. With eyes closed and bowed head, after a few moments Jennifer said, "I'm remembering the last time we went camping when I got stuck in my sleeping bag." She opened her eyes and told her aunt the story.

"On our last camping trip I woke up at night and couldn't find the opening to my sleeping bag. I was all turned around in the dark and I couldn't breathe very well. I was really, really scared."

"How long ago was that?" Cynthia asked.

"Last week," she replied.

"Well, let's have Jesus show the little girl from last week that she's not stuck in her sleeping bag anymore so she'll feel better."

"Okay," Jennifer timidly said.

"Imagine Jesus being in the sleeping bag with you when you were stuck," Cynthia guided.

"I can imagine it."

"What's Jesus doing?" Cynthia asked.

"He's making it really light in there and telling me I'm okay. I feel better with Jesus there. He's showing me how to get my head out of the sleeping bag."

"Can you imagine getting your head out?"

"Oh, yes," Jennifer answered, tears subsiding.

"Let's show little Jennifer she's not stuck anymore and a whole week has passed since that happened."

With Mom and Dad's help, Cynthia led Jennifer through a timeline of the week, selecting a memory for each day and waiting until Jennifer remembered the event. By the end of the first timeline Jennifer had stopped crying and was significantly less distressed.

"Let's do it again," Cynthia suggested and asked Jennifer to remember waking up in her sleeping bag all turned around.

"I remember it," Jennifer gently moaned.

"What's happening now when you bring Jesus into it?"

"This time I imagine him being in the tent and showing me my mom and dad are right there by me and they will help me if I need it."

"Good. And let's show her being stuck in the sleeping bag is over. Okay?"

Cynthia led Jennifer through another timeline, mentioning each day of the week and waiting until Jennifer thought of a memory for each day. At the end of the timeline, Cynthia reassured Jennifer that being stuck in her sleeping bag happened only once and it was all the way back to last week. Cynthia reminded Jennifer she could call out for help if she needed.

Jennifer, growing obviously sleepy, nodded in agreement.

"Let's do it one more time," Cynthia prodded. "Let's show Jennifer from last week she's okay and if anything bad happens during the night, like getting twisted in your sleeping bag, Mom, Dad and Aunt Cynthia will be right here to help you.

"Okay," she agreed, quietly resting on Mom.

"Can you see yourself in the sleeping bag from the last camping trip?" Cynthia asked.

"Yes," she acknowledged sleepily.

"Anything bothering you?"

"No, not really. I wish mom or dad would help me but they are asleep."

"What's Jesus doing?" Jennifer asked.

"He's helping me lay my head on the pillow. I want to go back to sleep."

"Can you see yourself going back to sleep knowing everything is okay?"

"Uh-uh."

"Let's show the pictures from the week again and then you can go to sleep."

Jennifer agreed sleepily. Cynthia mentioned each memory from the previous week and waited until Jennifer acknowledged the memory. By the end of the timeline she was noticeably tired from crying and the work of the Healing Timeline. Due to the neural integration that we suspect occurs with this method, individuals are often very tired after experiencing the Healing Timeline. By the end of the third repetition, Jennifer was nestled in her mother's lap, ready for sleep.

"Ready to get into your sleeping bag?" her mother asked. Jennifer nodded and fell right to sleep.

The family camped for three more nights. Jennifer did not have any difficulty at bedtime for the remainder of the August trip or on camping trips that followed. When Cynthia discussed the Healing Timeline experience with Jennifer's parents, they remembered Jennifer telling them about her problem in the sleeping bag on the morning after it occurred, but neither of them associated her current distress with the earlier experience. It was only during the Healing Timeline the connection was made. By reassuring "the Jennifer-from-seven-days-ago" that her problem was over, the current distress about falling asleep on the August camping trip was resolved. Jennifer was obviously afraid to get turned around in her sleeping bag again, but she was not able to clearly communicate this concern to her parents. Even if she had been able to express her fear, their reassurances would probably not have enabled her to completely release her anxiety.

The wonder of the Healing Timeline is evident in this story. Through prayer, the Holy Spirit led Jennifer to the right memory for healing and the timeline integrated the memory until it was fully resolved.

Children have wonderful success using the Healing Timeline. Unlike some adults, they rarely have trouble imagining Jesus in the memory scene. Children who have not had any religious background are almost always capable of seeing Jesus or an angel in the earlier memory. Like Jennifer, they usually resolve their issues quickly and are often quite tired when finished. They bounce back quickly, though, and enjoy lasting relief from problems resolved through the Healing Timeline.

Connor's Camping Trip

Connor's camping trip was not quite as fun as Jennifer's outing. Every summer Conner's family went camping with two other families from their church. The families began camping when the kids were young. After a decade of their summer tradition, the oldest child in the group was fifteen and the youngest child age seven. The adults were best friends and the kids were like extended family to one another. A lot of trust developed in the three families over time so there was no alarm when Connor, age nine, and the oldest boy Zachary, age 15, asked if they could take a short walk down to the river together. Connor's dad agreed, on the condition the boys took a walkie-talkie radio with them and were back at a specific time.

When they got near the river, Zachary, who had been carrying the walkie-talkie, turned it off and placed it on a nearby rock. Connor noticed this and said, "My dad will be mad if he finds out we turned off the walkie-talkie."

"It's out of batteries," Zachary lied. "We'll tell him when we get back. Plus, I want to show you something that only big kids know about."

Zachary proceeded to sexually molest Connor. Within the allotted time, the boys walked back into camp and Zachary placed the walkie-talkie on the camping table Connor's dad was busy elsewhere and the boys separated to their own tents.

The next day, after they were home, Connor told his mother about the abuse. He was afraid he would be in trouble because they had turned off the radio. Connor told her he kept asking to carry the walkie-talkie but Zachary insisted he was older and should be the one to carry it. Connor felt ashamed of himself for many things, one of which was that he did not tell his dad right away about what happened. When they learned of the incident, Connor's parents called the police and reported their best friend's son.

To help Connor heal from the molestation, they contacted their pastor, who suggested Connor meet with someone from the church prayer team. Team members had been trained in the Healing Timeline and the pastor assured them he had seen more healing through the method than any other counseling he could recommend. Connor's dad spoke with the prayer counselor Mark the night before Connor's first appointment, giving him details of the incident. Bit by bit, Connor had told his parents about what happened on the walk to the river with Zachary.

When Mark and Connor met, Connor was reluctant to tell about the problem on the camping trip. They had never met before and Connor was embarrassed and ashamed about what happened. Mark kindly reassured Connor he wouldn't need to tell the story in order to heal the "Zachary problem." He assured Connor his dad had given him enough information for them to begin and Jesus would lead them to the rest. Connor tentatively agreed to close his eyes and imagine Jesus joining him at the river when he was there alone with Zachary.

"Can you see Jesus there with you?" Mark asked.

"Yes," Connor replied, obviously very uncomfortable about what happened and embarrassed to be remembering the scene in front of Mark.

"What is Jesus doing?" Mark asked.

"He's telling Zachary to stop it and he's making him stop. I feel scared. After he makes Zachary stop he tells me it's not my fault," Connor said.

"That's right," Mark affirmed. "Zachary is the one who made this happen and it wasn't right. I'm sorry it happened to you. Of course you were scared. That's normal."

Mark led Connor through a timeline from the camping trip that happened four weeks previously by using a memory from each week. Mark wrote the cues down as Connor remembered them to serve as a cue sheet. Mark guided Connor to remember the scene five times with Jesus, followed by the written cues. By the end of the session, Connor was less distressed and relieved he didn't have to tell Mark the story. He became a little more talkative and said, "I'm beginning to work this out in my mind. I'm still a little afraid but I feel better. I wish I had told my dad right away."

"Why didn't you?" Mark asked.

"Because Zachary told me not to, and I didn't want my dad to be mad about the radio and stuff."

Mark commended Connor for telling his mom the next day. "You did the right thing by telling your parents," he confirmed. "How are you feeling about the Zachary thing now?"

"I feel tricked by someone I know. I'm a little bit scared and I hope I won't see him again, but I feel a lot better after Jesus helped me today."

The next week Mark and Connor met again. Connor still did not want to talk about what happened at the river with Zachary, but he told Mark in the beginning of the session his most upsetting feeling was fear it would happen again. Mark guided Connor to invite Jesus into the memory scene and listen to what he had to say. He reported Jesus told him it would not happen again because Connor knew he could say no and if anything bad like that started to happen he could tell his parents right away. There was no blame on Connor or reason to be ashamed for what Zachary did. Together Mark and Connor used the timeline five times.

During the second session, between timelines, Connor shared phrases like, "My head went blank. "If he tries it again I'll have the courage to do what's right," and, "I'd like to beat up Zachary and throw him to the bottom of the river." These statements represent the normal emotional progression that occurs through the Healing Timeline. "My head went blank" speaks of the confusion a victim feels when violated by someone they trust. A victim cannot comprehend and manage the thoughts and emotions associated with their violation so they "blank out" as a form of dissociation. "If he tries it again I'll have the courage to do what's right" speaks of Connor's powerlessness beginning to resolve. Children are powerless victims when they are abused. Connor's remark reflects he is regaining a sense of personal power by generating problem-solving ideas should something like this happen again. It tells the counselor the issue of powerlessness is being healed. Connor could imagine himself speaking and acting on his own behalf if the scenario with Zachary reoccurred. And "I'd like to beat up Zachary and throw him to the bottom of the river" is Connor's expression of anger. Although his Christian family would not actually support Connor's idea, it is a healthy sign he was moving through the normal layers of the trauma. By the second session of the HTL, Connor moved through the confusion, being frozen, the issue of powerless, and into anger. Eventually all victims move into anger and it is a sign they are coming to life again after a trauma.

During the third and final session two weeks later, Connor said, "If Zachary called to apologize to me I wouldn't talk to him. He has nothing to say to me. I wouldn't want to talk to him or see him again. I'm kind of scared, but if I could, I would tell him how I felt. I wouldn't believe him or trust him."

In the final session, Connor's disturbance about the incident itself was almost completely gone and he focused on the aftermath of the trauma like telling his parents and talking to the police. Connor had the choice of going to court as a witness or giving a private testimony to a police officer. He had chosen to speak privately to the police officer. During the final Healing Timeline session, Connor imagined Jesus with him in the scene where he gave his testimony to an officer. He reported it made him feel better to imagine Jesus being there with him and Mark led him through a timeline proving the legal stuff was over and he wouldn't have to do it again. Connor was greatly relieved at the end of the session and felt he didn't need to see Mark anymore to heal the "river problem with Zachary." He said, "I don't think about it anymore. I used to worry about it every night and now I don't think about it."

After the incident with Zachary, Connor became withdrawn and was very afraid he might see Zachary at school or church and not know what to do. After three sessions using the Healing Timeline, Connor understood the problem was over, it was not his fault, and he knew how he would handle something like this if it ever occurred again. It is impressive that Connor, on his own, planned the empowered response of telling Zachary how he felt if he should encounter him. Mark's conversation with his dad confirmed the healing Connor was reporting.

Two months after the Healing Timeline sessions, Connor's dad contacted Mark requesting documents for the court case. He said Connor continued to be open and outgoing like he had been before the molesttion and the withdrawn, frightened behavior that immediately followed the incident went away after the three HTL sessions. Connor was still participating in the sports he enjoyed and had actually encountered Zachary at church and handled it well. He told his dad he didn't want to be friends with Zachary anymore, and the family assured him he did not have to re-engage their friendship. Zachary had written Connor a letter of apology that the family accepted, but they also continued to press charges as they were instructed by the police. Zachary had exhibited other sexually deviant behaviors before the incident with Connor, and the police wanted him to confront and deal with his problem.

Connor's story of healing is one of my favorite testimonies to the Healing Timeline. I love it because a child's life was healed within weeks of the abuse he experienced. Due to his healing, Connor will not have to go through years trying to overcome misplaced shame and guilt due to Zachary's behavior. He will not constantly replay the scenes in his mind of Zachary turning off the walkie-talkie and then hate or berate himself. Without the Healing Timeline, it is likely Connor would have developed strategies for covering up or managing his shame. Those childhood strategies could easily have lasted a lifetime. Invariably, Connor would have blamed himself for some part of the situation like the radio being turned off if he had not revisited the abuse scenes with Jesus and heard Jesus' truth spoken into the problem.

The repetitions of the timeline integrated Jesus' truth where the lies and shame were beginning to take hold.

The confusion Connor initially felt during the molestation could have turned into repetitive dissociation. Instead, Mark helped Connor integrate the confusion so it will not be re-triggered later in other settings.

Due to the Healing Timeline, the powerlessness Connor legitimately felt in the abuse situation will not become a pattern of feeling victimized in future relationships. If Connor and Mark had not addressed the powerlessness of his abuse, Connor would probably find himself in other male relationships where he would feel victimized or powerless. It is common for feelings related to a trauma to repeat over and over until they are healed. Talking about a trauma does not appear to sufficiently remove its emotional triggers. Not only is talking insufficient to remove the emotional triggers, confronting Zachary and pressing charges would also have been insufficient to heal the internal confusion, powerlessness, shame, and anger Connor felt. Using the HTL, Mark and Connor integrated and resolved feelings which could have repeated for years. Due to their work together, it is plausible Connor will not ever re-trigger his feelings from the experience with Zachary.

Abused children feel bad and often start acting like 'bad' children. It would have been normal for Connor to withdraw from a sport he loved after the Zachary incident or to withdraw from his teammates due to the secret he was carrying. Connor will not have these problems because he told his parents about the perpetrator's behavior, they believed him and provided an effective healing opportunity for recovery.

Many people were sexually abused as children. When they receive Jesus' healing and repetitions of the timeline, they are astounded about the impact the abuse has had on their lives. For years they have lived with erroneous, negative views of themselves which they carry into lifestyle and relationship choices. Healing a child's abuse at the point where it occurred means he or she will continue to grow and develop as God intended, not in the shadow of evil abuse. I wish for children all around the world to receive this method for healing as soon as possible so they will know their abuse was not their fault, they did the best they could, and God's love and truth is restored to them for the past, the present, and the future.

Nine

Lie Versus Truth: Failing in Mathematics

Scotty's story is another case where a child was saved years of heartache due to the Healing Timeline. A recurring situation led him to believe a lie about himself. Using his eleven-year-old brain, Scotty surmised there was something significantly wrong with him and his behavior matched the lie Scotty believed. No matter how hard he worked, Scotty was not able to get different results until he replaced the lie with truth and integrated it with the Healing Timeline.

Don't we all believe lies which influence our behavior? Growing up with imperfect parents in a broken world, all of us carry wounds and erroneous beliefs about who we are and what we deserve. Many of these beliefs came to rest in our hearts as children when we used childish thinking to make sense of our experience in the world. Shifting these internal beliefs, at the places where they occurred, is possible through the Healing Timeline. The truth brings us freedom, especially when it is applied to the origins of a lie. Scotty's case study is an example of changing a belief at its root and seeing lifelong results.

Scotty's Story

Scotty was finishing his math homework in the back of the public school classroom with four other students from fifth grade. Because they were gifted in mathematics, the classroom teacher had the five students working independently in an accelerated math program with the teacher's oversight. They were finishing a mathematics textbook two grades above the classroom level. The main classroom was working from the fifth grade textbook and the students in the back of the room were finishing a seventh grade math book. It was spring and the five dedicated students were pushing themselves and each other to complete the seventh grade math curriculum before the school year turned into summer vacation. Scotty was one of the highly motivated math students.

When school started in the fall, and each of the students would enter sixth grade, Scotty was scheduled to leave public school and attend a private Christian school. He was reluctant to change schools and leave his classmates, but he was also looking forward to the more challenging curriculum the private school offered. When the fifth grade year ended, with the confidence from successfully finishing the seventh grade math book, Scotty said to his mother, "I should be ahead in math when I go to my new school. We finished the seventh grade book and I'll be going into sixth grade at my new school. I should be one year ahead."

Scotty's mother tried to give him a different perspective. "That might be true," she agreed, "but sometimes private schools move at a faster pace or use a different math program. You might be just at grade level in math when you enter, or you might even be a little bit behind. You'll be able to do the work, though," she encouraged him.

Scotty did not worry over the summer. He knew he would do well when he started at his new school and math was one of his favorite subjects. Understanding math concepts came easily to him and the work was not very challenging in the advanced math group at the back of his public classroom. In public school the math was fun and easy.

In the fall, Scotty began school in his new classroom at a private school. There were several challenges, one of which was maneuvering new relationships with peers and the teaching style of the new curriculum. Most of the students in the classroom had been in the school since kindergarten and knew each other. They were also very accustomed to the pace of learning and the homework expectation for each night. Unlike his experience in public school, at his new private school Scotty was expected to complete a math assignment at home each evening and make corrections to the assignment from the day before. Other class subjects were assigned as well. The teachers in his new school expected at least ninety minutes of homework each day. Peers in class corrected each other's homework, including the corrections from the previous day's assignment. Scotty fell behind with his math work and other subjects. His parents encouraged him to do his best and reminded him that it would take a while for him to adjust to his new school and its learning expectations.

Although math generally was easy for Scotty to understand, his quarterly report cards were marked with C's for mathematics. His parents tried to help where they could, but Scotty explained he was understanding the material and was doing his best. He was invited to participate in optional projects for gifted students, which led his parents to believe he was still demonstrating his normal level of academic ability. Over the course of the year he gradually made friends and seemed to be adapting fairly well.

In the spring of the sixth grade all students were administered a mathematics placement test for entrance into junior high school. Scotty scored in the average range for mathematics and was tracked on the average course for junior high placement. His parents did not pressure Scotty to perform at a level beyond his ability, but it seemed curious to them a student who had at one time been a very successful math student would be considered "average" and placed accordingly for junior high school and beyond.

Wanting to encourage him, Scotty's parents validated his ability and assured him he would be successful wherever he was placed.

In eighth grade mathematics, Scotty's grades continued to be average for the mid-level math program. On his quarterly report cards his other subjects were marked A's, but in mathematics Scotty was achieving B's and C's. In the middle of the year he remarked to his mother, "I'm embarrassed that I'm not in the upper math program."

Surprised by the statement, she asked him to explain.

"I remember when I was good at math but now I'm bad at it. I thought I would be in the upper math track, for sure. But ever since sixth grade I've been a failure at it."

"A failure?" she questioned. Scotty's mom knew he had some challenges adapting to the new math curriculum in the private school, but she did not have serious concerns regarding his grades.

"Yes, I'm a failure at it now," he confirmed.

Since B's and C's are not failing grades, she pressed further. Scotty described a scenario from sixth grade, which he had never mentioned to her before. He said, "My teacher had a chart on the wall with everyone's grades on it. I remember looking at my grades and seeing F's (failing grades) on the row for my math grades. Every time I didn't do my corrections from the previous day's math homework, I got an F. I wasn't used to making corrections from my public school so I often forgot. I had a lot of F's next to my name and everyone could see them. I figured out I was a failure."

Scotty's mom was surprised. Scotty had been quite successful adapting to a new school and she had no idea he had formed this severe critical judgment of himself. "Is that what you think now in eighth grade?" she asked.

"Yes," Scotty admitted. "I'm not good in math anymore."

Scotty's mom could not believe that her son who had easily succeeded in math had reached the limit of his ability to perform well. Although she did not pressure him to get top academic marks, it concerned her that he had made the determination in his heart he was a failure.

Her friend Linda was on the prayer team at their church and had told Scotty's mom about the Healing Timeline. "Would you be willing to pray about this with our friend Linda?" she asked. Scotty agreed.

When the three of them met together, Scotty's mom briefly described his story to Linda. "Let's see what Jesus has to say about this," Linda suggested to Scotty. "Would you be willing to let him go anywhere inside of you to fix this problem?" she asked.

"Yes," Scotty confirmed. They asked God to direct their session and Linda coached Scotty to say a silent prayer asking God to go anywhere he desired inside and to show them where to go in Scotty's memory to fix the problem of feeling like a failure. After a few quiet moments Linda asked Scotty what he was thinking about.

"I'm remembering standing in front of the grading chart in sixth grade and seeing all those F's next to my name. I thought to myself *I'm a failure in math.*"

"Can you imagine Jesus being in the scene with you as well?" Linda asked.

"Yes, I can see Jesus there."

"What is he doing or saying?"

"Nothing, he's looking at the grades with me. He's standing in a way that blocks other kids from seeing the grades."

"How does that make you feel?"

"Better," Scotty continued. "I remember feeling like I wanted to sink into a hole in the floor when everybody was standing around looking at the grades and I had F's. With Jesus standing there no one else can see my grades."

"Is he saying anything to you?" Linda asked.

"Yeah," Scotty replied. "He's telling me I'm not a failure. He's the one who made me good at math and I'm still good at it. That was just a tough time and I was getting used to the work at my new school."

"Now let's prove it's over, okay? Are you looking at the grading chart in the fall, winter or spring?"

"The winter," Scotty answered.

"Okay, then, think of something that happened in the spring that year."

Scotty nodded he could remember something from spring. "I played soccer with the Falcons," he said.

"Good. Now remember something from the summer. Did you take any trips?"

"Yeah, we went to visit my Grandma in California that summer."

"Okay, now think of something from right before school started in seventh grade."

"Got it," Scotty answered.

"And then get a memory for the middle of seventh grade, maybe something you got for Christmas."

"Okay."

"And now remember something from the summer between seventh and eighth grade. "

"I remember," Scotty said.

"And something from the middle of eighth grade."

"Uh-uh." Scotty nodded.

"And then remember getting your report card last week in eighth grade math."

"I got it," Scotty answered.

"Is it okay if we go right back to the sixth grade memory?" Linda asked, and Scotty nodded it was fine.

"What do you feel now when you see yourself looking at the grades on the wall before Jesus is there?"

"Definitely not as bad," Scotty replied. "I'm still

embarrassed I had all those F's but now I understand why I
had them. I wasn't used to making corrections every night.
I guess it was more of a correction problem than me being
bad at math. I wasn't doing what I was supposed to do."

"Would you bring Jesus in again?"

"Yeah, I can see him there. He's put his arm around
me and is blocking the other kids again. He says, 'I made
you good at math and you can learn from this. It's going
to take some time to learn the ways of your new school but
then you're going to be very successful. He says he's proud
of me for trying and doing what I can do.'"

"Does that make you feel better?" Linda asked.

"A lot better," Scotty sighed. "I thought there was
something wrong with me and I would always be bad at
math. I guess that's not really what happened. I didn't think
of this before."

"Right," Linda confirmed. "Let's go through the pictures again and prove that being a new sixth grader and trying to figure out how to do the math homework everyday
is over. Think of something from the spring, like playing
soccer with the Falcons."

"Got it," Scotty answered.

"And taking the trip to California in the summer."
Linda waited until Scotty acknowledged the memory and
then continued with the rest of the cues up to the present,
waiting between cues until Scotty acknowledged he had
recalled a memory.

Returning to the memory for the third time Scotty said, "I understand that I'm not a failure at all. I was having trouble doing math corrections every night. We don't have to turn in corrections for eighth grade Algebra and I completely understand the math now."

"It's not too challenging for you?" Linda asked.

"No, I just don't do my homework now."

Rather than engage in a conversation concerning his current math class, Linda coached Scotty to invite Jesus into the sixth grade image of looking at the grades on the wall.

"I can see him with me and he's telling me that I'm a really great kid and this whole problem is over. He's right. I figured it out. I'm not a failure."

His mom later said she could sense Scotty letting go of the idea he was a failure during the last image with Jesus. "I sensed the change in his body," she remarked. His words and demeanor were evidence of the shift. She said, "It was as if Scotty carried around a bag with the word "Failure" on it until that moment with Jesus when he set it down."

Linda led Scotty through a final timeline from sixth grade to the present. When she mentioned spring, Scotty quickly pointed out he was asked to be part of an accelerated learning group that did a special bridge-building project during that quarter. The teacher had said, "Since you're such a good analytical thinker, I thought you would like to be involved in the bridge-building enrichment class." This positive memory spontaneously emerged on the third timeline after Scotty had stopped thinking of himself as a failure.

They continued through the timeline up to the present. Linda checked to see if any distress remained for Scotty when he thought about looking at his grades in sixth grade.

"No, not really," he answered. "I feel fine about sixth grade. I wish I had scored better on the math placement test so I was on the advanced track now. When they gave us the math placement test in sixth grade I left a whole bunch of answers blank. I thought, *Who cares? I'm a failure anyway.* I didn't even try to do well on it."

His mom later said she had always wondered why Scotty had scored poorly on the placement test. She did not expect him to be an over-achiever, but his performance did not appear to match his ability. She was reluctant to bring up the subject with Scotty because she did not want to discourage him any further. His remarks about leaving test questions blank explained his low placement score.

After one session of the Healing Timeline with Linda until he graduated from high school, Scotty received almost all A's on his report cards in math. The very next quarter he had an A in eighth grade math rather than a B-. His performance immediately changed after their work together. Something very significant shifted in Scotty's heart: he returned to believing the truth.

Scotty's behavior changed when his belief changed.

When he thought of himself as a failure as evidenced by the F's which his peers could see on the sixth grade wall, Scotty acted in accordance with his belief, which was reflected in his math scores. By the end of eighth grade the belief was well internalized and he did not expect himself to excel in mathematics. His parents encouraged him that he was still a capable math student, but their words did not override the concrete experience of seeing F's next to his name. The seeds of a negative belief were planted in sixth grade by a very specific, ongoing circumstance which had taken root and was growing in Scotty's heart.

In telling the story later, Scott said, "I remember having F's in sixth grade and feeling terrible about it. It didn't matter how badly I wanted to improve. I had really tried and not seen any results. I felt like there was no way out; I couldn't do it anymore. It was really disheartening."

Referencing the change after the Healing Timeline, he continued, "In ninth grade I was so far ahead I took my tests in ink because I knew I wasn't going to make any mistakes. I remember finishing the final exam in about 30 minutes. It wasn't a very easy final for the majority of the class, but I totally nailed it."

His mom said, "I often wonder what would have happened if Linda had not used the Healing Timeline with Scotty to heal the lie he started believing in sixth grade. We had no idea he was thinking of himself as a failure. We always thought Scotty would grow up to be an architect or an engineer. He was constantly making buildings with craft sticks and toy bricks. As a young man he builds bridges with an engineering team."

The comments from Scotty's mom express the heart and soul of the Healing Timeline. When people change what they believe in their hearts they consequently change their behavior. Parents usually have no concept of the way children are internalizing beliefs about themselves based on their experiences in life. The Healing Timeline reconnected Scotty to the truth which Jesus planted in his heart regarding his spiritual gifts and talents and his outcomes changed.

Ten

Summary

A New Normal

By adding a timeline to prayer counseling, clients' lives will be permanently healed on a deep level. They will think, feel, and spontaneously live differently after a counselor has led them through enough repetitions of a timeline. The Healing Timeline is an intervention which takes clients to a new level for "normal."

Day by day, as life occurs for each of us, difficulties, trials, and suffering get added to our experience of the world. These challenges shape who we are and what we consider normal for living. They are not difficulties we would choose to experience, but after we have lived through wars, sexual abuse, neglect, and trauma they become part of the internal psyche and are normalized in our experience of living.

An analogy for this concept is the idea of a wagon

slowly moving across the landscape. The wagon, our life, comes pre-loaded with gifts, talents, and purpose. As it progresses, people and circumstances put other things on the wagon. Some of the contributions are positive but others are negative. Contributions that cause shame will make the wagon very heavy to pull. Whatever has been added to the wagon, by choice or circumstance, positive or negative, will become part of the wagon owner's view of normal. An outsider can look at the load and wonder, "Why are you carrying that around?" The wagon owner, who might have been quite young and powerless when negative things got added, may not know he's carrying burdens that are weighing him down. He may have grown up in an environment that did very little to support or enhance the positive content of his wagon. The collective goods on his wagon become his identity.

The Healing Timeline will enable clients to remove content from their metaphorical wagons. When individuals come for counseling they are essentially saying, "I'm having trouble pulling my wagon around. Something is wrong. I'm not being successful in life and relationships." Through prayer, we ask the Holy Spirit to show us what is causing the particular problem the client is trying to solve. He shows the client where to go on the wagon to remove unneeded baggage the client has picked up on life's journey. Jesus' intervention and timelines are the method for removing the unwanted goods once they have been identified. Removing items from the wagon will allow clients to base their identities on the original preload of gifts, talents, and purpose rather than the collection of unwanted experiences they themselves, or others, have added to life's load. Removing the unwanted beliefs and experiences empowers clients to redefine what they consider normal by changing what they internally carry through life.

After the Healing Timeline, a "new normal" emerges for clients. People tend to choose circumstances and relationships that match their internal world. When the internal world (a client's wagon load of experience, belief, and identity) is changed, they naturally move into more positive environments for living. Others also respond to them differently. Outsiders can see and sense to a certain degree what we carry on our wagons and relate to us based on our internal view of self. Lightening our load through the Healing Timeline will naturally lead to better life experiences because we will be drawn to people and opportunities that match our more positive internal state.

For instance, forty-one-year-old Francis was sexually abused when she was three years old. In the first session addressing the abuse with the Healing Timeline, she said, "I can't believe the choices I have made with a wrong view of myself because of this. When I go through the timeline, I can see choice after choice I made based on the view of myself after the abuse. I could only go so far in trusting men until I became closed. Even though two of the men wanted to marry me, I never said yes because I couldn't trust them. It had nothing to do with them." Using the wagon metaphor to consider her comments, the sexual abuse that got added to Susan's load caused her to steer away from long term, intimate relationships into isolation. After the Healing Timeline, she chose a relationship with a safe, kind man. Susan moved in a positive, new direction after her internal changes.

The question might be asked, "Why look into the past when the client's problems are in the present?" Some therapies specifically avoid considering the past and focus solely on achieving present day solutions with clients. This is not a bad or ineffective path to choose. However, the human self is a collection of experience, thoughts, beliefs, natural gifts, and resources. All these components combine when "the self" makes a decision or approaches a problem. By using the Healing Timeline to change earlier beliefs that formed within, clients change the foundation upon which they base their ideas for problem solving.

In the New Living Testament, 1 Corinthians 13:11 says, "When I was a child, I spoke and thought and reasoned as a child does. But when I grew up, I put away childish things." The childish methods used for problem solving include fantasy, pretending, denying, ignoring, lying, acting out, people-pleasing, over-compensating, excessive "good behavior," and other childish tools. Unfortunately, children are truly powerless to solve most of the problems they face, many of which are caused by the adults in their lives.

Children can be trained to solve their childhood squabbles and sibling rivalries, but many children are the victims of serious adult problems. They live in conditions with fighting, divorce, domestic violence, sexual abuse, addictions, poverty, wars, verbal abuse, prejudice, etc. In these cases, which are always beyond the scope of their problem-solving realm, children must find ways to endure or lessen the pain in which they are raised. In order to survive, they draw on their childish methods. They may learn to pretend something bad isn't happening through fantasy or use a childish attempt to make something better. Children will try to take care of drunk, addicted parents in order to make things better for themselves. They can get very good at their childish coping skills. When children from bad situations grow up, they carry their foundational methods for problem solving within them.

It can be very difficult to put away "childish thinking and reasoning" as scripture suggests when it has become part of a person's main strategy for survival. A child who goes into the fantasy world of books or pretending in her abusive childhood home will be well-practiced at ignoring serious problems when they occur in her adult life. She may tolerate violence and domestic abuse for herself and children because her own childhood method of denying problems guides her to ignore intolerable situations. Solving current problems by healing yesterday's hurts is necessary because adults are often using their childish problem-solving methods disguised as adult thinking.

Every childhood problem-solving technique has an adult version. In reverse, every ineffective adult problem-solving method has a childish root. Adult versions of childish thinking are excessive drinking, drug use, pornography, or anything that will help clients live in denial and avoid facing the truth of their situations. Like children, through these methods adults can sustain a form of avoidance for years. Sometimes children choose positive behaviors as problem solving methods. In adults, this appears as perfectionism, over-working, excessive care-taking, and codependence. It is probably not too strong to suggest that all adult dysfunctional behavior is rooted in childish reasoning. Therefore, in order to solve current adult problems, we need counseling methods that equip people to release and revise their childish ways. Going into the past and healing a memory with Jesus, then integrating the changes through the timeline, provides such a method.

The Healing Timeline is an intervention that will produce change whether it is implemented sooner or later in life. By showing clients that their negative experiences are over and reinstating truth where lies have entered, they are equipped to live in their gifts and strengths rather than false, negative views of themselves. Scripture says, *"As a man believes in his heart, so he is."* (Proverbs 23:9) Whether lie or truth, a person's beliefs are formed in the heart layer upon layer and experience upon experience. The Healing Timeline gives us a way to enter the layer where a belief was laid down and correct it with the loving presence of Jesus. We hypothesize the timeline integrates the change throughout the heart and mind. Captives are set free when they believe the truth.

A preacher once said, "God takes the ghetto out of us; then we take ourselves out of the ghetto." All of us carry the ghetto inside. It is the sin and evil in the world we have inherited, internalized, and proliferated. God takes the ghetto out of us by changing our emotions and beliefs until they match his truth. When we are in alignment with his view of us, we make choices and changes for life and well-being. The Healing Timeline is a process that positively changes our thoughts and emotions. By following the steps outlined in this chapter, we can participate in the work of taking the ghetto out of God's people. When internal changes have been made, people take themselves out of the ghetto.

Instructions

Eleven

Step-by-Step Instructions

"When I was a child, I spoke and thought and reasoned as a child does. But when I grew up, I put away childish things." 1 Corinthians 13:11 (New Living Translation)

The Healing Timeline is comprised of three basic steps, which will be broken down into very specific instructions in this chapter. In review, the HTL is accomplished by (1) asking God to guide the client to a memory related to a current problem, (2) inviting Jesus into the memory scene, and (3) proving the problem is over with repetitions of a timeline. The timeline is repeated until no distress remains in the memory scene. When the memory scene is resolved, clients are able to address their presenting problems with new insights, solutions, and resources.

Instructions for the steps are presented in two ways. First, a list of steps is provided in a succinct form which can be used as a checklist or basic guide for moving through the HTL. Secondly, the directions are repeated in paragraph form to further expand understanding of each step. The most important reminder when using the Healing Timeline is to **keep repeating the timeline** until no distress remains in the memory scene. Most memories will fully resolve with the HTL if enough repetitions are completed. It is a disservice to the client to begin the emotional work of firing the neurons related to a painful memory and then leave him or her in the painful memory without sufficient resolution. Repeating the timeline up to ten times or more should bring relief to the client. As a general guideline, it is important to keep going once the Healing Timeline has begun.

Summary Instructions for
The Healing Timeline

1. The counselor begins the session with prayer.

2. Discussion of the presenting problem or selecting a memory.

3. Prayer—Client gives God permission to go anywhere he desires in the conscious or unconscious of the client.

4. Prayer—Client asks God to lead them to the right place for healing.

5. Invite Jesus to enter the memory scene. If the client cannot "see" Jesus enter, proceed with the timeline after the counselor says something like, "This was really hard but it's over. Here's the proof."

6. If the client can see Jesus enter the scene, the counselor asks, "What do you see Jesus doing or saying?" Then the counselor asks, "Can you imagine Jesus saying, 'This is over and you're not stuck in this situation anymore?'" (Or something similar.)

7. Timeline. Client's eyes are closed, counselor's eyes are usually open. The counselor leads the client through a timeline of spontaneous memories for every year or reads memories from the client's cue sheet up to the present.

8. Counselor asks the client to go back into the memory scene without Jesus present and asks, "What is happening now?" This will change with every timeline. After the client has briefly described the scene and identified the main feeling, invite Jesus to enter the scene again. Repeat step five.

9. The counselor leads the client through the timeline again. Take a break and/or discuss.

10. Return to the memory scene without Jesus pres-

ent and clarify the current scene and the primary distressing feeling. Invite Jesus into the memory scene. Repeat step five.

11. Repeat the timeline. More negative memories will surface in the initial timelines, but the memories will grow increasingly more positive with every repetition.

12. Keep returning to the memory scene until there is no distress for the younger self in the memory scene or the client says something like, "I can't imagine being in that situation anymore." Expect complete relief from the memory scene. Partial relief means the work is not done.

13. After all distress is clear in the memory scene the counselor may lead into forgiveness prayer, breaking soul ties, deliverance prayer, etc. if appropriate.

14. Revisit the presenting issue. Sometimes the client will immediately have new ideas to solve the current problem and other times solutions will evolve. Change always occurs in the client's life through the Healing Timeline.

15. Inform clients they will probably be tired after the HTL and need to take special care when driving, etc. The brain continues to reorganize itself after the session, so clients may temporarily feel emotional, dissociated, hungry, and tired.

Expanded Instructions for The Healing Timeline

Step 1. Counselor Opens the Session with Prayer

As Christian counselors, our goal is to follow God's direction during a prayer counseling session. By opening with prayer, the counseling team is inviting God to direct the healing process and lead the counselor and the client throughout their work.

Step 2. Discussion of the Presenting Problem

The purpose of step two is to hear the client's story with empathy and clarify the main source of difficulty. The challenge for prayer counselors is to resist the urge to make their own insightful connections to the client's problem before God has led them through the Healing Timeline. In order to effectively employ the Healing Timeline, prayer counselors should help clients identify their current problem and move into the prayer of asking God to guide them.

Clients come for healing prayer because they are seeking solutions to their problems. It is common for them to already have discussed their difficulties with family members, pastors, doctors, and mental health professionals. Everyone, including prayer counselors, usually has ideas about ways to solve the client's problem. Clients often come with diagnoses and few solutions to heal their diagnoses. The goal of the Healing Timeline, and specifically step two, is very different than the problem-solving of traditional counseling. Prayer counselors should avoid over-talking about the problem so they do not neglect prayer and the timeline process. If clients could easily follow the advice others readily give them, they would probably not be in the position of asking one more person for help. God can help people, and we can help facilitate the client's connection with God through this method. The timeline changes people on the inside, who then change their lives on the outside. It is important to move through step two, talking about the current problem, respectfully and relatively briefly.

In a two-hour prayer counseling session, discussion of the presenting problem should take less than 30 minutes. Prayer counselors need to communicate they have a sympathetic understanding of the client's problem then guide the process toward inner resolution, not long discussions. With experience, prayer counselors learn nothing they say equals the resolution that occurs through the Healing Timeline. They also learn that any worthy advice is better heard after the internal changes have been made through the HTL process, rather than before the inner work has been done.

Alternately, the HTL may also begin with a specific, remembered incident. Sometimes clients bring a specific memory into prayer counseling. In this case, the Healing Timeline work can begin at the memory age the client suggests instead of discussion about a current problem. For example, a client might begin by sharing that she was sexually abused at age eight and was seeking healing for the eight-year-old memory. The client and prayer counselor say the customary prayers and then proceed directly into the memory from age eight. The client briefly describes the remembered incident to the counselor, identifies the main feeling, and invites Jesus into the memory scene, then follows the remaining HTL steps.

Step 3. Prayer Part One: The client gives God permission to go anywhere he desires in the conscious or unconscious of the client

Apart from the actual repetitions of the timeline, this is the most important step in successfully using the Healing Timeline protocol. Giving God permission to go anywhere in the conscious or unconscious of the client is critical because the Holy Spirit knows the perfect place to begin healing the client's current distress. By giving God permission to enter the hidden places, the client will be guided into memories or related issues that might otherwise have been bypassed. The Holy Spirit is gentle and respectful. He will not enter where he is not invited to search. In order to obtain optimal results, clients must give God permission to seek anywhere within themselves to find the essential source for healing.

If preferred, the opening of the counseling session can combine the prayer in which the counselor invites God to be present in the session, followed by inviting the client to pray, silently or aloud, giving God permission to go anywhere within for healing.

By client and counselor yielding the process to the Holy Spirit, healing will begin at exactly the right place. The importance of this step cannot be overstressed. Anything less than God's guidance can be frustrating and insufficient. By asking the client to yield his or her consciousness to the search of the Holy Spirit, the HTL process will flow and be successful.

Step 4. Prayer Part Two: Client asks God to lead them to the right place for healing

Modern science tells us a major portion of our knowledge, memory, and beliefs are below the level of conscious self-awareness. Since the majority of memory is held outside conscious thinking, we ask God to reveal the necessary memory for healing. Clients will not always choose the right memory for healing by relying solely on their left-brain self-reflection. Therefore, we guide the client to ask God where he would like to lead them for healing the present concern. Usually, it is better for the client to pray this prayer rather than the counselor. After the client has prayed the prayer, internally or aloud, they wait silently (generally with eyes closed) until the client acknowledges he or she senses God has led to a specific scene or time in the client's life. The counselor then asks the client to open his or her eyes and briefly describe the scene. The discussion should be brief. Here again, problem solving is not the goal.

Before Jesus is invited into the memory scene, the client is asked to identify the main feeling or describe the scene. Each time the client returns to the memory scene, he or she will be asked to name the main feeling or distress. By asking about the memory scene *before* Jesus is brought into the memory, the layers of the problem which need healing can be identified. If Jesus is always in the memory scene, the feelings will be affected by his presence. For example, if a child was asked to take the household garbage outside on a dark night he would have one feeling by himself and a different feeling if he were accompanied by a trusted adult. In this step we are looking for the organic feelings which were present when the difficulty occurred. These will be harder to identify if Jesus is invited into the memory scene too early.

After the main distress or feeling is identified, the client is often very emotional about the memory. Do not linger at this point or try to minimize the distress. It is much more effective to witness Jesus in the scene and begin repetitions of the timeline. The timelines will permanently lower distress, which is more powerful and longer lasting than trying to soothe clients in the moment. Counselors should be empathetic and kind, but move directly into repetitions of the timeline.

Step 5. Invite Jesus to Enter the Memory Scene

The counselor guides the client to invite Jesus into the scene he or she is remembering. Jesus is omnipresent and not limited by time. John Loren Sandford said, "For us, time is like a book. Today is the page we are on right now, and we can only be in today but Jesus can go anywhere in the book—forward or backward." Time is not the same for Jesus as it is in our earthly lives. He can represent himself in time at any point. Although the client probably did not experience Jesus in the memory the first time it occurred, he was present and available to help. By inviting Jesus to enter the memory as it is currently being recalled, clients can see, hear, and understand the experience from Jesus' perspective. He is always truthful, compassionate and wise. This step is common to most inner healing prayer models, which are a useful resource for step five.

In this phase counselors must be sensitive to the client's experience of Jesus in the memory. Are they experiencing him in a way consistent with scripture? Jesus does not shame, criticize, or belittle people. He does not want harm for the humans he created. Counselors must monitor this intervention to make sure clients are not putting their own erroneous beliefs onto the person of Jesus. If a client says, "Jesus wanted to punish me because I was really bad...." the counselor must intervene with a gentle phrase like, "This does not sound like the Jesus we know from the bible."

If the client cannot imagine Jesus entering the memory scene, proceed with the timeline after the counselor says something like, "This was really hard but it's over. Here's the proof." After one or two repetitions of the timeline, the client is usually able to have some experience of Jesus in the memory scene by sensing or feeling him, even if Jesus cannot internally be "seen" Sensing or feeling Jesus' presence is sufficient for the intervention in the memory scene. The client's awareness of Jesus may increase with several sessions of the Healing Timeline.

Emotions are generally quite activated when clients begin to recall the memory scene. It is helpful for the client and counselor to know the primary emotion of the remembered event, but it is not necessary to process the emotions by talking about them. For some counselors this will go against their training to help clients analyze and expand their feelings. Due to the hypothesis timelines change brain neural networks, it is more important to move into the timeline phase rather than encourage deeper development of the client's emotions. It can be difficult to say to a person who is crying, "Think of a memory at age six..." instead of a sympathetic, consoling response. The positive outcomes from using the timeline will reinforce the importance of bypassing the traditional step of more and more emotion. It is better to change the brain than have the client continue to cry about the problem.

Step 6. If the Client Can See Jesus Enter the Scene: The counselor says, "What do you see Jesus doing or saying?"

The counselor listens while the client describes what Jesus is doing in the memory scene. This can include Jesus taking the client out of the bad situation, saying something supportive or helpful, or responding to the aggressor in an appropriate, empowered way. This intervention will always be consistent with the Jesus we read about in the Christian bible or it is not a real representation of Jesus. As mentioned previously, the counselor is responsible for making sure the Jesus experienced by the client is consistent with the Jesus we read about in scripture. Witnessing Jesus' interaction in the memory scene may take several minutes in which the counselor waits quietly while the client observes Jesus and listens to him. This is primarily an experience the client observes internally, which is reported to the counselor. Occasionally the counselor may ask, "What is happening now?" At an appropriate time, the counselor interjects, "Can you imagine Jesus saying something like, 'This situation is over and you're not stuck here anymore'?" The counselor waits until the client nods in agreement. The counselor can suggest other very brief phrases that Jesus might say based on the main emotion the client identified when he or she returned to the memory scene. The main feeling of the memory scene will change with every repetition of the timeline.

It may seem odd for the counselor to prompt Jesus about what to say in the memory scene. Because clients are emotional when remembering the scene, they are not always able to perceive Jesus correctly or with spiritually sensitive minds. Occasionally clients will say, "I can see Jesus but he is not doing or saying anything." Well-grounded Christian counselors can safely suggest loving, helpful phrases which meet the need for the client and reflect the true, loving nature of Jesus. The main feeling the client identifies at the beginning of each memory scene should be sensitively addressed before the timeline, either spontaneously by Jesus or by t he counselor who asks, "Can you imagine Jesus saying…?" and then inserts a statement which validates the main feeling.

For example, if the client identifies the main feeling in the memory scene as betrayal, before the counselor guides the client into the timeline, and after the client has observed Jesus' spontaneous interactions in the memory scene, the counselor would make sure the client has heard some validating, truthful phrase about betrayal. Truth and validation are very powerful for healing. The counselor needs only to ask, "Can you imagine Jesus saying he did not want you betrayed? What happened here was wrong. It's over," followed by the timeline.

It is important to insert truthful phrases *where the injury took place,* which is being re-witnessed in the memory scene. By recalling a memory scene, clients are activating the brain neural networks that hold the original memory. Speaking into the part of the brain which experienced and stored the memory is the right place to insert the healing words of truth and validation. If a client had a damaging experience at age ten, he or she will have the greatest opportunity for healing if the words of Jesus are spoken into the ten-year-old brain that processed the memory when it first occurred. Identifying the main feeling and addressing it in the same neural network is the goal of the Healing Timeline. This age-based repair is followed by the timeline to integrate and make the change permanent.

Step 7. Timeline

The timeline begins when the counselor asks the client to remember a real memory from his or her life beginning one year after the memory scene, followed by subsequent memories up to the client's current age. If the memory scene is at age ten, the timeline will begin with age eleven. The counselor leads the client by saying, "Think of a memory at age 11 (counselor pauses until client nods), age 12, age 13, etc., until the client's current age is reached. The client does not tell his or her memories to the counselor during the timeline but rather nods or signals that a memory has come to mind. No matter how distressing the memories are, the client and counselor do not stop to talk about the memories during the timeline. The purpose of the timeline is to create neural integration, which is enhanced by steadily progressing through the client's ages. Clients generally keep their eyes closed during the timeline and the counselor's eyes are open.

It is recommended that the client prepare a written list of brief, neutral memories which the counselor can read as an alternative to saying the client's ages for the timeline. The counselor and client can prepare this list together or the client can prepare it apart from the counseling session. To use the cue sheet, the counselor reads the memory such as, "Remember when you got your red bike," (the cue written for 11), wait for a nod, then, "started seventh grade at Rosemont," (12 year old cue), "ran track in 8th grade…" (13 year. old cue) continuing to the present. Spontaneous memories will also occur for the client with the use of the written cue sheet. The purpose of the written list is to make it easier for the client to move through the timeline.

Using the written timeline or speaking the client's actual age is preferred over the use of calendar or school years. Reading the cue or mentioning the client's ages throughout the timeline will generally evoke a personal memory. If the counselor guides the timeline by using calendar years such as 1987, the client may remember news

from that year or some other detached piece of information. Calendar years tend to produce left-brain, analytical
memories. If the counselor uses school years for prompts,
such as "sixth grade, seventh grade, etc." the client will be
predisposed to remember events associated with school
and not access their full range of memories. In the HTL, it
is best for the client to recall spontaneous memories which
are left-and-right-brain based. Clients will naturally select
the appropriate memory when prompted with their age or
given a cue from the written sheet.

Regarding the memories in the timeline, the question
is often asked, "Does the client have to be in each memory
or show them to the younger child?" The answer is no, the
client only needs to have recollection of a memory related
to the time period. It is not necessary to "show" the memories to the younger self or work to imagine the client being
in each memory of the timeline. For example, if a client is
prompted with the written cue, "getting a new dress for
graduation," she will spontaneously remember something
near the event, but she does not have to see herself re-expe-
riencing any aspect of graduation. In this example, it would
be common for the client to remember her dad got a new car
about the same time she graduated. Generally, the spontaneous memory will be related to some aspect of the original
memory scene or the client's presenting issue. The written
cue, "new dress for graduation" could produce the spontaneous memory of Dad getting a new car in one session. In

a different session with a different memory scene, the same written cue might lead to a spontaneous memory such as "my boyfriend broke up with me over the summer." Simply recalling events in a time period will fire the necessary age-related neurons for a successful timeline.

Negative memories, which have a similar tone to the memory scene, will be the first to appear during the timeline. With each repetition the timeline moves from negative to increasingly more positive memories. Clients may have to be reassured that negative memories in the beginning are a good sign neural integration is occurring. For example, a memory scene which contains rejection may be followed by a timeline with rejection memories in it. Three or four timelines later, the memories in the timeline may not contain any rejection memories. Instead, feelings of inclusion an acceptance may spontaneously appear.

It is not necessary to use every year of the client's life for each timeline. The goal of the HTL is to repeat the memory scene/timeline sequence enough times to completely reduce the client's distress when remembering the memory scene. Completely reducing distress is accomplished by many repetitions of the timeline. In order to accomplish three to ten or more timelines in a given session, it is acceptable to alternate even years and odd years during a timeline. If possible, the counselor should prompt with each age until 20, but may shift to alternating years afterward. Later in the session, when the client's distress has been significantly reduced, the counselor may choose to use five-year increments during the timeline. As a general principle, it is better to employ more timelines with increments than fewer timelines using each of the client's ages.

Another common, related question is, "What do we do at the end of the timeline?" At the end of the timeline (client's current age), the client may open his or her eyes for a brief break. There is no specific step taken at the end of the timeline other than to take a short break or return to the memory scene. It is not necessary to take a break after each timeline, but after two or three cycles of the memory scene/timeline sequence the client usually needs a brief moment for resting. A lot of emotional material and insight may occur for the client during the timeline. The counselor must pace discussion with the client at the end of the timeline with the goal of completing as many timelines as needed during the session. As a reminder, the purpose of the HTL protocol is to create permanent healing through neural integration via the timeline. The counselor and client do not want to spend too long in discussion during the break and forfeit the opportunity for the deepest level of the client's healing.

If a trauma is recalled during the timeline, the counselor can assure the client that the trauma will be written down to be specifically addressed at a later time. Once a session has begun with a memory scene, the counselor and client do not shift focus until the original memory scene is completely clear of distress even if a more upsetting event is remembered. Counselors need to trust that the Holy Spirit led them to the right memory in the beginning of the session. Switching memory scenes during a session can be a method for avoiding the pain of a remembered event.

The timeline is the essential healing element of this protocol. It can bring results which heretofore have not been experienced through talk therapy alone. A counselor using the Healing Timeline method must commit to using the timeline repeatedly once the process has begun until the client's distress is virtually erased from the memory scene. This is an uncommon outcome for standard therapy but an expected occurrence in every session using the Healing Timeline. Repeating the timeline properly will set captives free.

Sample Cue Sheet

Birthday_____   Current Age_____

Year	Age	Memory
1993	5	kindergarten at West Side
1994	6	playing soccer at recess
1995	7	swimming birthday party
1996	8	summer trip to San Francisco
1997	9	best friends with Pat
1998	10	got a new mountain bike for Christmas
1999	11	summer camping trip with Hendersons
2000	12	started Jr. High at Mountain View

To read from this sample cue sheet, the counselor would begin one year after the age of the client's memory scene. If the client's memory scene was at age eight, the counselor would begin reading the memory cues at age nine by saying:

"Remember your best friend Pat." (written cue from age 9) *Pause until the client acknowledges a memory has been recalled.* "Got a new mountain bike for Christmas." (cue from age 10) *Pause.* "Summer camping trip with Hendersons." *Pause.* "Started Junior High School at Mountain View."

The counselor reads cues up to the client's current age at which point they return to the memory scene or take a brief break and then return to the memory scene.

Step 8. After a Brief Break (optional): The counselor asks the client to go back into the memory scene without Jesus present

Up to this point, the client should have finished one timeline after viewing the memory scene with Jesus present. Now the counselor asks the client to view the memory scene again briefly without Jesus present. As mentioned previously, the client will have a different response when remembering the incident as it actually occurred, versus seeing the scene with Jesus present. Without Jesus in the memory, the counselor asks, "What is happening now?" Due to the neural integration, the client's answer will be different each time he or she re-enters the memory scene after a timeline. The counselor is listening, in part, for the shift in feelings which will occur through each repetition of the timeline. Once the client has briefly described the memory scene, he or she invites Jesus to enter the scene again.

After inviting Jesus to enter the memory scene for the second time, the client watches and listens to Jesus' intervention. This is a live, dynamic interchange in the Spirit. Observing and listening to Jesus' spontaneous interactions is important. During this time, the counselor is prayerfully silent or may occasionally ask, "What do you see Jesus doing, etc." After a few minutes, the counselor may insert, "Can you imagine Jesus saying…?" (choosing a phrase that validates the primary distress as identified by the client in this section) followed by, "Can you imagine Jesus saying, 'This is over'?"

For important phrases to insert see *Guidelines* later in this chapter. The counselor needs to be compassionate, kind, truthful, and sensitive to the Holy Spirit about what to say to the client. Validating the main distress in the memory scene is the critical component to this step.

Step 9. Repeat Timeline

The counselor leads the client through another timeline by stating the client's age or reading the cue sheet beginning one year after the remembered incident. When the client's current age is reached, the counselor and client may take a break with brief discussion or return directly to the memory scene again.

Steps 10, 11, 12. Return to the Memory Scene: Repeat timelines until there is no distress for the younger self in the memory scene

The miracle of the Healing Timeline is the phenomenon that a client can be very upset about a memory when it is first recalled through prayer and 30 to 60 minutes later be calm and insightful about the same memory due to neural integration. When clients recall a memory scene, they activate the brain neurons which hold the memory and systematically rewire them to the rest of the brain, decreasing distress. The Healing Timeline is not complete until repetitions of the timeline have virtually eliminated distress in the memory scene. Counselors need to expect complete relief from the memory scene. Partial relief means the work is not done.

The counselor must decide when the memory scene/timeline series is complete by assessing for congruent emotions and statements from the client. When clients begin to receive relief from a distressing memory, they often believe they are done when the memory is only partially clear. After being very upset about an injustice they have carried for a lifetime, after a few timelines clients will say something like, "It feels so much better...." which. in fact, the memory does. The work of the Healing Timeline is not finished, though, until the memory feels completely better and the client fully understands the difficulty is over. When clients experience partial relief from a long-held memory, they are grateful and do not yet understand they can experience complete relief. A common error in using the Healing Timeline is to not make enough repetitions of the memory scene/timeline sequence.

It is impossible to accomplish too many timelines for a given memory. With each repetition of the timeline, the memories get increasingly more positive and give clients greater insight and positive feelings about themselves. For best results, it is necessary to clarify the main feeling in the memory scene, bring Jesus in, validate the feelings and repeat the timeline until there is no distress in the memory scene.

The progression of feelings in a memory scene follows a general pattern. Depending on the severity of the memory, a client's emotions often progress from being numb or in shock to grief, hurt, anger, confusion (ex. "How could my mother stand by and let my step-dad beat me?") to concern for others and relief. Children often start with the feeling of confusion followed by the same sequence of emotions. Until the client reaches the feeling state of relief the work of the session is not complete. Relief will be evidenced by the client no longer crying and being upset. He or she will say something like, "I really understand now that it's over," or "I can't imagine being in that situation anymore."

Another way to conceptualize the pattern for the HTL is to consider it in four sections. The first phase could be considered the Frozen Phase when the client cannot see or hear Jesus in the memory scene. The memory and its associated feelings are emotionally frozen and difficult for the client to access. The antidote for the Frozen Phase is the same for all phases – gently, or more directly, guide the client through repetitions of the timeline. The four-phase pattern is like a bell curve. The Frozen Phase is the beginning of the bell curve when the client begins the timeline process.

The second phase is Confusion, which occurs when clients are trying to mentally resolve why something painful happened to them. They may be trying to reconcile their role in the difficulty or the motives of others whose actions hurt them. As mentioned previously, children are always confused about the hurtful behavior of others and they assume something bad about themselves must have caused others to treat them poorly. This phase is the upward movement toward the peak of the bell curve.

At a recent HTL training, my friend and prayer partner Corky Morse, shared two questions, which she finds very helpful for leading clients deeper into the healing process. One of them applies directly to the Confusion Phase. After a few timelines enabling clients to access the memory scene, she asks, "Would the child (or younger self of the adult) like to ask Jesus a question?" Clients generally have an important question for Jesus. His answer enables them to begin mentally reconciling a troubling memory. Jesus gives them very important information, which helps them understand their problem. Clients are often surprised to find things were very different than they understood them to be when the difficulty occurred. Hearing Jesus' perspective on a problem or his answer to an important question is helpful to clients. A young woman, whose parents allowed her to travel with an adult male friend who molested her, asked Jesus, "Why did my parents let me go with him? Didn't they care about me?" Jesus' reply explained the full situation to her, which enabled her to understand it more fully and forgive them after the HTL process.

The third phase, which could be considered the peak of the bell curve, is the Deepest Pain of the memory. After the initial timelines, the brain and body appear to open the neurons that hold the stored and unprocessed feelings of a memory. After the initial two to five timelines, clients may start sobbing because they are fully accessing the memory. Guiding them through several more timelines will resolve their deep distress. If Jesus cannot be seen or felt in the memory scene, the counselor needs to simply guide the client through a few timelines until the client becomes more stabilized. Here again, it is important for the counselor to remain calm and confident that the timeline process will fully resolve the client's deepest pain, no matter what it may be. Having used this process in hundreds of counseling sessions, I have not seen an exception to this outcome. Timelines will resolve client's deepest distress if enough timelines are employed. It might be tempting for a counselor to stop and comfort a client if hard crying begins, but the timelines will resolve the crying if the client is guided through enough timelines.

Corky's second important question is appropriate to ask at this stage. When crying lessens, she asks clients, "What did your younger self need?" A client generally knows what he or she needed, and is able to name something important they have lived without for a long time. Acknowledging their need temporarily touches their deep pain, but Jesus wants to satisfy all of our needs, and is capable of doing so in the memory scene. Jesus can provide the very things people are missing in their lives. Having him provide these during the replay of the memory scene is transformative to clients. Following this healing with timelines integrates his restorative touch and leads clients into peace and relief.

The fourth and final phase, on the 'downhill' side after the peak of the bell curve, is the Relief and Understanding Phase. This too, requires several timelines. After the most intense emotion has passed, clients feel relief and gain understanding. They will have increasing insight with every timeline. If time allows, it is important to give the client an opportunity to grasp as many new perspectives on the problem as possible. In this phase, each time clients re-imagine themselves in the memory scene followed by timelines, they will gain additional insight about themselves, others and the origins of their problem. In the case study, Rebels in the Congo, Tresor's younger self wanted to see the timeline images over and over. It reassured him that his war trauma was over, he and his family were safe from the threat of being captured, and a lifetime goal of attending college had been fulfilled. His younger self wanted to repeatedly experience all the good news. If a short time remains after clients have entered into the Relief and Understanding Phase, they can be reassured that new thoughts and perspectives will keep emerging for them outside the session. Weeks after a HTL session, clients gain new perspectives and shift their behavior in response to timeline healing.

Sometimes a memory is too complex to be completely resolved in one session. Emotional distress should decrease throughout the session, but occasionally a topic is not fully resolved in the counseling time. Counselors should plan ninety minutes to two hours for a session using the Healing Timeline. If six to 15 timelines have been repeated and the distress is not fully resolved, counselors should reassure clients they will finish the work next time they meet. Often the memory continues to resolve between sessions.

To continue an unfinished session in a follow-up meeting, the counselor would ask something like, "When you think about the memory we were working on last time, what do you feel now? Is anything still unresolved about it?" The counselor waits quietly while the client imagines the same memory scene and evaluates to see if any distressing feelings remain. If no distress remains in the memory (not just partial relief), the memory continued resolving between sessions and the work is done. If the client identifies a remaining emotion, the counselor guides the client to invite Jesus into the scene and they continue the memory/timeline sequences until the client is completely relieved of any distress in the memory scene.

It is common for aspects of a presenting issue to be addressed in more than one session. Each session will typically bring full relief to the memory scene, but a topic and its various aspects may be covered in a series of sessions. For example, a man struggling with an alcoholic wife would present one aspect of the problem in the beginning of counseling. The counselor and client would ask Jesus to lead them to the right place to begin healing this issue in the client's life. Five sessions later, the client may still be focusing on alcoholism in his family, but he may be more acutely aware of its impact on the children and his inability to protect the children from their mother. With this specific focus, Jesus would lead them to a different memory, which would probably be resolved in the session. A common occurrence is for one session to completely relieve the distress for a specific memory scene but for a complex presenting issue to be addressed more than one time.

Many repetitions of the memory scene/timeline sequence are required to achieve full healing for the client. The counselor is in the best position to judge when this has been accomplished by the emotions and comments from the client. The work of the HTL is not finished until the client experiences complete relief from a distressing memory. In most cases, this will happen in one session if the counselor guides the client through enough timelines.

Step 13. After All Distress Is Clear in the Memory Scene: The counselor may lead into prayers of forgiveness, etc.

By first using the HTL in a session, counselors are able to help clients lower their distress about a remembered event, which makes it easier for them to pray forgiveness prayers for their offenders and themselves. After the Healing Timeline has been used, counselors can proceed to inner healing protocols such as breaking soul ties, deliverance, and forgiveness prayers.

All actions taken after the HTL will be more grounded in a peaceful, stabilized client. There is significantly less resistance in clients who understand their difficulty is over through changing their brains via the timeline. Deliverance prayers flow more easily when the client is not holding strong emotion toward an offender or situation. Inner healing techniques will be more easily accomplished after the Healing Timeline. The case study *Pastors Need Help, Too* is a good example of this process. When a client is asked to forgive an offender and replies, "I can't bring myself to do it…" the Healing Timeline counselor says, "That's all right for now," and proceeds through another timeline. After the emotion has subsided through repetitions of the timeline, the counselor may ask later," Are you ready to forgive now?" and receive the client's effortless reply, "I already did it with Jesus." The Healing Timeline does not replace inner healing prayer. Instead, it moves the outcomes from inner healing prayer to new levels, making for long lasting and easier-to-achieve results.

Step 14. Revisit the Presenting Issue

Change always occurs in the client's life through the Healing Timeline. Sometimes the client will immediately have new ideas to solve the current problem and other times solutions will evolve. If time remains in the session, the counselor and client can revisit the topic of the client's presenting issue. The counselor can ask a question such as, "When you think about your problem with _____ (the reason they come for counseling) what are you thinking/feeling now?"

Over time, the client will always respond to his or her presenting issue differently. At the end of the memory scene/timeline sequences clients can be very tired and not thinking clearly about the presenting issue. When the brain integration completes over the following days, clients will spontaneously think about their problems in new ways. They may be able to articulate new ways of thinking at the end of a session, or they may need time to let the integration take place. Refocusing on the presenting issue in a session is optional, depending on time and the ability of the client.

Step 15. After the Healing Timeline

The work of the HTL is very taxing on the client's brain. The repetitions of the timeline require effort, focused attention, and a good supply of brain fuel. After the HTL, clients' resources are often depleted and they may feel tired, hungry, and somewhat dissociated. It is helpful for the counselor to inform clients they may not feel quite like themselves for a day or so after the session. The HTL can temporarily dysregulate clients. Having a snack after the session and allowing themselves to rest will enhance the client's recovery while the brain continues to re-structure itself.

Guidelines for the Healing Timeline

As discussed in Step Six, Jesus is invited into the memory scene and the client watches and listens to his intervention, followed by the timeline. The memory scene/timeline sequence should occur five or more times in a session. Before the session is complete, there are important phrases that may need to be inserted into the memory scene. The following phrases are truths the client will probably need to hear during the session or over the course of counseling. It is not necessary to use every phrase in every session, but generally these statements reflect what clients need to hear in order to heal their painful memories. It is likely Jesus will spontaneously speak these truths. If not, the counselor should be sensitive to insert them by asking, "Can you imagine Jesus saying...?"

1. Important Phrases for the Memory Scene

When choosing phrases for the memory scene, some or all of these could apply:

a. "It's over."

b. "It was not your fault."

c. "You did the best you could."

d. "Children are powerless to solve grown up problems."

e. Validation of the younger self's problem and feelings. Ex. "You're right. You should be mad. This would make anybody mad."

f. "You're not a victim anymore."

g. Jesus saying, "I love you."

2. Maintaining Momentum

Jesus was kind and compassionate to prostitutes, tax collectors, and common folk. We need to be compassionate and truthful when we as counselors are invited into a client's memory scene which may be ugly and unpleasant, filled with mistakes and wrongdoing by clients and their offenders. We have no record of Jesus shaming people for their mistakes and wrongdoing. We do not hear him say to people, "You should not have done that. What were you thinking!?" Occasionally Jesus spoke the truth in anger to the Pharisees, but by nature Jesus is always loving, patient, forgiving, and seeking to restore people to wholeness. Counselors must follow his lead in the Healing Timeline process. Harshly judging victims and offenders will not portray the real Christ to hurting people who have come for healing. Even offenders are people created by God who need transformation. This does not mean we minimize wrongdoing, but berating and judging offenders will not create openness to healing. God is the only righteous judge. A counselor's role is to guide the process so clients experience truth, validation, and restoration, which prepares the way to forgiveness, deliverance, and freedom. Please do not tell people what they should have done or felt. Validation and compassion are the keys to transformation through the Healing Timeline.

Just as it is not helpful to judge or berate people in the memory scene, it is equally harmful to 'spiritualize' away the true pain people have experienced. A counselor can quickly shut down the healing process by intellectualizing or minimizing a client's suffering, by asking clients to deny their pain for a lofty, "spiritual" reason, and other insensitive ways of responding to clients. It is not uncommon for parents whose children have died to hear, "It was for the best. This is God's perfect will." Comments like these do not belong in the Healing Timeline protocol. Clients will be able to better understand their suffering over time. Counselors can help them move toward deep spiritual awareness with Christ's compassion and understanding. After clients have released their pain through the Healing Timeline, they are usually able to grasp their suffering in new ways. HTL counselors must be careful to let this depth emerge over time for the client, and not spiritualize the client's problem with the counselor's theology.

3. Progression in a General Pattern

The client will become aware of the mental and emotional

contents of the memory scene in layers. Each repetition of the memory scene/timeline sequence will expose another factual or emotional component of the memory. Generally, the feelings in the memory scene begin with the client feeling frozen, very emotional, or something in between these two extremes, then progresses to confused, scared, mad, sad, lonely, and relieved. Because the focus in the memory scene changes with almost every timeline, it is useful for the client to clarify the most significant aspect of the memory each time he or she returns to the memory scene. Jesus' spontaneous words or prompts by the counselor will be a response to the significant aspect of the memory scene.

Another general pattern is the level of emotion through the timeline. The beginning repetitions of the memory scene/timeline sequence will often be the most emotional, with decreasing emotion as the timeline progresses. Eventually, the client will begin to see positive, internal resources as he or she progresses through the timeline for the same memory scene, which at one point caused tears. For this reason, it is very important to keep moving through memory scene/timeline repetitions until emotion has significantly decreased.

The pattern of the Healing Timeline is similar to a bell curve. Through prayer the client is guided into a memory, the emotion of the memory increases, peaks, then drops to a neutral or positive level. Integration through the timeline is the operative intervention that causes this pattern.

Counselors can expect to see this pattern in all Healing Timeline sessions.

4. Notice What's Going on Inside the Counselor

Does the client's situation make the counselor feel sad, angry, and powerless? These are clues to the feelings of the client. Counselors need to be creative and attentive to problem solving with Jesus. Is the counselor receiving a word of knowledge from the Holy Spirit? A word of knowledge is insight about the client's problem or memory scene the counselor would only know if revealed by the Holy Spirit directly to the counselor. When the counselor and client have given God permission to direct the session, it is likely they will experience God's insight coming directly into their own spirits. When this happens, the counselor needs to share this information with sensitive timing and humility. It is recommended that the counselor keep this information quiet for a while to see if the client moves towards understanding it on his or her own. When a client first sees the memory scene, the identified emotions may be shock or hurt. The counselor may be aware of other feelings the client is feeling, but these may be outside the client's current awareness. Over time, through repetitions of the timeline, clients will discover for themselves their feelings, which the counselor may have known for quite a while. The sensitivity and humility of the HTL process directs counselors to wait until a word of knowledge is revealed to the client or to share it with tentativeness.

Sharing a word of knowledge can be done by saying some phrase such as, "I was wondering if you felt _____?" and inserting whatever the Holy Spirit has revealed to the counselor. If the client disagrees, even if the counselor is confident of what he or she is saying, the counselor must not try to convince the client of the counselor's perspective. If the counselor is correctly hearing from the Holy Spirit, the word of knowledge will become evident in time. Words of knowledge are meant to be helpful to the client and counselor, not arguing points or places of distraction. Their purpose is to communicate understanding from God to the client. When shared with humility and grace, they can be very powerful contributors to the client's healing. Without counselor sensitivity, they can also hurt the client and shut down the client's openness to restoration. As a guiding principle, it is better to wait when sharing a word of knowledge rather than proceed too quickly or too ardently when God has revealed something to the counselor.

5. Limitations of the Healing Timeline

As mentioned previously, the Healing Timeline is specific for resolving real, concrete memories. Usually the client is guided to a real memory through the prayer process or he or she might ask to heal a painful, remembered event, in which case the client describes the memory to the counselor and then invites Jesus into the memory scene. Following this practice will bring great relief to many people.

The Healing Timeline is not adequate to heal traumas that are held completely outside the consciousness of the client. When clients cannot remember certain periods of their lifetime, it is a clue they are holding painful memories in a dissociated way. Dissociation is the term for holding memories or emotions out of accessible awareness. If a client cannot remember or access any memories from certain years, those years are said to be 'dissociated.' Dissociation is a protective mechanism that helps us survive what we cannot tolerate at the time. The Healing Timeline is not sufficient to excavate and heal dissociated memories. For example, if a client says she was abused but cannot remember when or by whom, she will need interventions beyond the application of the Healing Timeline.

Some clients have had severe abuse starting at very young ages. God has given us the ability to completely shut out memories that are too painful to tolerate. Trying to resolve these with the Healing Timeline will open the emotional pathways that hold the painful memories but not completely heal them because the memories are not completely known. Using timelines and only achieving partial resolution can be harmful to the client. It may leave him or her distressed without awareness of which other memories to heal because the rest of the memory is dissociated.

Another limitation of the HTL is that it is only appropriate for memories after age two. Concrete memory begins to form at approximately two years of age. The type of memory formed before age two is different than the picture-like memory that develops later. The Healing Timeline requires concrete, picture-like memories that Jesus can enter and replay, speaking his truth and wisdom into the situation. The Healing Timeline is too limited to bring relief to traumas before age two, but Lifespan Integration can heal preverbal memories and dissociation.

6. Refer for Professional Help. Many problems are outside the scope of the Healing Timeline

The Healing Timeline is an intervention that can be added to any situation where Christian counselors would apply inner healing prayer. There are other Christian counseling situations where the HTL can be used successfully, but there are many situations and problems which are beyond the scope of the Healing Timeline. Counselors should refer clients for professional help with eating disorders, multiple personality diagnosis, depression, suicidal thoughts, etc.

An unstable client is not a good match for the Healing Timeline. The timeline appears to disorganize and then reorganize the brain. If a client is already very destabilized, guiding them through many repetitions of the timeline can temporarily further destabilize them. It is assumed that lay counselors would ordinarily refer destabilized clients or severe diagnoses for professional help. Professional counselors could be trained to use Lifespan Integration with depression, dissociative identity disorders, eating disorders, and more, but these conditions are beyond the application of the Healing Timeline. Professional and non-professional ethics require that counselors work only within the scope of their training. The Healing Timeline has limited application and should be used primarily with stable clients in a prayer context.

The Healing Timeline Worksheet

Client's Current Age: _____

1. Counselor opens with prayer and leads client to give God permission to go anywhere he desires in the conscious or unconscious of the client.

2. Discussion of the presenting problem or selecting a memory (Do not try to solve the problem through conversation):

_____

_____

_____

_____

_____

_____

_____

3. Prayer — Client asks God to lead to the right place for healing. Wait silently. Client describes scene to counselor. Age in memory scene: _____

_____

_____

_____

_____

_____

218

_____

_____

_____

Memory and Timeline 1

4. Invite Jesus to enter the memory scene. The Counselor says, "What do you see Jesus doing or saying?" Client describes what is seen. If necessary, the counselor says, "This bad situation is over and you're not stuck here anymore?"

5. Timeline. Client's eyes are generally closed, counselor's eyes are usually open. Counselor generally begins by using the written cue sheet of the client's timeline beginning one year after the age in the memory scene. Without a cue sheet, the counselor may lead the client through a timeline by counting the client's ages up to the present. Some clients will not need a cue sheet and will get spontaneous memories on their own without cues. For the timeline, do not use calendar years such 1998, 1999 or sixth grade, seventh grade, etc.

Memory and Timeline 2

6. Counselor asks the client to go back to the memory scene without Jesus present and asks, "What is happening now?" Counselors listens for the main distressing feeling.

_____

_____

_____

_____

_____

_____

7. Bring Jesus into the memory scene. The counselor asks, "What is Jesus doing or saying?" If necessary, the counselor asks, "Can you imagine him saying...?" (using content that validates the information above and other appropriate remarks).

8. Proceed through timeline.

Memory and Timeline 3

9. Counselor asks the client to go back into the memory scene without Jesus present and asks, "What is happening now?"

_____

_____

_____

_____

_____

_____

10. Bring Jesus into the memory scene. Observe and listen to Jesus in the memory scene.

11. Proceed through timeline.

Memory and Timeline 4

12. Counselor asks the client to go back into the memory scene without Jesus present and asks, "What is happening now or what is the younger-self feeling?"

_____

_____

_____

_____

13. Observe and listen to Jesus in the memory scene.

14. Proceed through timeline.

Memory and Timeline 5

15. Counselor asks the client to go back into the memory scene without Jesus present and asks, "What is happening now?" Counselor listens for feelings.

_____

_____

_____

_____

_____

_____

_____

_____

16. Observe and listen to Jesus into the memory scene.

17. Proceed through timeline.

Closing

18. Check to see if there is any distress remaining in the memory scene for the younger self. If even a small amount of distress remains in the memory scene, repeat memory scene and timeline sequence. After the timelines are complete, prayer counseling can proceed to:

A. Forgiveness prayers, breaking of soul ties, deliverance prayer, etc.

B. Discussion of the current, presenting issue.

C. Debrief the Healing Timeline experience. Inform clients that they will probably be tired for a day or two after the HTL because the brain is continuing to reorganize itself after the session.

Twelve

Using the
Healing Timeline
in Ministry Settings

A ministry that employs the Healing Timeline needs to have suitable counselors and appropriate clients. Not everyone is a good candidate to implement or receive ministry through the Healing Timeline. A commonality appeared in interviewing ministry programs that use the method. Generally, they had similar criteria for selecting counselors and common requirements for clients. Their comments about the effectiveness of the Healing Timeline were unanimous.

Dr. Trish Treece, a leader in ChangePoint International ministry in Auburn, Washington described their success with the Healing Timeline as remarkable. She said, "When helping clients work on particular issues, I see a greater effectiveness when we add the Healing Timeline. We get a double effect in terms of quickness, ease, and greater freedom for clients in the present." Their ministry includes in-depth prayer work, teaching on overall identity in Christ, forgiveness, warfare, etc. She continued, "The inner healing component of the ministry has greatly benefited from the Healing Timeline in terms of the stronger results we see." ChangePoint International currently has a year-and-a-half waiting list for healing prayer through their ministry.

An individual counselor who had been involved with inner healing prayer for ten years said, "I will never go back to the traditional form of inner healing prayer. When I came upon the Healing Timeline it made a huge difference in the speed and the level to which people are healed. It's a deeper and more permanent healing. Because healing happens so quickly, the client is amazed at the truth they've just found out, and application of the new truth enters their lives right away. It's easy to see the changes in their lives immediately."

Rev. Terry Tripp, Pastor for Congregational Care at First Presbyterian Church in Bellevue, Washington said, "The Healing Timeline is amazing. Since we have begun using the Healing Timeline, request for our ministry of healing prayer has tripled." These two ministry leaders and other prayer counselors gave their input on the components that make up a successful prayer ministry using the Healing Timeline. In most cases, healing prayer ministries were already in place when the counselor or director learned the technique of the Healing Timeline. Through practice they have developed guidelines that are worthy to be shared with others.

The Counselor

An individual counselor can use the Healing Timeline with a client, but in most healing prayer ministries a team carried out the counseling with a designated leader. The team model is not a requirement for using the Healing Timeline, but was a common practice in the ministries I interviewed. The criteria for suitable prayer counselors included:

1. Spiritual Maturity in a Personal Relationship with Jesus Christ

A counselor using the Healing Timeline needs to be a Christian. Since Jesus appearing in the memory scene is an integral step in the process, it is necessary for counselors to have an ongoing relationship with Jesus Christ. Spiritual maturity as a Christian is critical for Healing Timeline counselors. It is imperative for them to know Jesus and scripture well enough to ascertain if the Jesus being reported in the memory scene is authentic and consistent with scriptures.

Counselors need to be experienced enough to know that God can be trusted to lead the process when asked, and that they, the counselors, do not need to direct, "sermonize," or control what happens. Counselors who cannot resist the urge to give clients advice when they should be quietly waiting and watching for the Holy Spirit's actions are not suitable as Healing Timeline counselors. Prayer counseling is not based on a formula. It is a live interaction between clients, counselors, and the Holy Spirit. Being able to trust the Spirit, which comes through maturity and practice, is vital to effective prayer ministry.

In order to maintain the capacity to hear Christ in the prayer counseling session, counselors need to spend ongoing personal time in bible study and prayer. A leader in the Bellevue, WA program said, "It's important for me to spend time daily in the Word—the Old and New Testament. The Word is the truth; that's how we know what God's truth is. I can't imagine being able to hear God's voice if I wasn't spending time with him everyday."

Spiritual and emotional maturity is also demonstrated by the capacity to accept another person's pain and suffering with compassion. Sometimes the client's pain can activate painful memories inside the counselor. Healing Timeline counselors need to be able to engage with the client's story while managing their own internal reactions. It is not helpful for a client to tritely hear from a counselor, "Oh, the same thing happened to me and this is how it worked out..." Sometimes minimal self-disclosure from the counselor is appropriate, but generally the session should be focused on the client's emotional needs. The counselor's capacity to manage his or her own affect is critical for moving the client through the stages of the session. Counselors can hear very difficult information in a session using the Healing Timeline. Their emotional stability is necessary for successful work with the Healing Timeline.

2. Counselors Need to Have Done Their Own Healing Work

Mature, experienced counselors will have much more to offer if they have sought out healing in their own lives. Those who have experienced healing are often best suited to offer healing. Personal transformation is a multi-layered, ongoing process. Counselors who have delved into the layers of their own psychological pain will have greater resources to provide others and they will have some understanding about psychological concepts.

Rev. Terry Tripp summarized their ministries' most important counselor criteria with these words, "Our best counselors have done their own work. They have led in inner healing prayer for a while. They can be genuinely honest about who they are and have a level of spiritual maturity demonstrated by their ability to trust God in their prayer sessions. They don't go into prayer with an agenda for someone." There are many forms of healing work. Counselors wishing to employ the Healing Timeline may have experienced other modalities for healing, but they should also have successfully experienced the Healing Timeline. Personally experiencing the HTL as a client will prepare counselors for the emotional power of the tool. It is not possible to comprehend or guide the level of emotion, insight, and change that occurs through the HTL unless the counselor has personally experienced it. The Healing Timeline will free up emotionally stuck places in the counselor, making it possible for him or her to deepen the work for the client. It is highly recommended that the counselor experience the Healing Timeline in preparation for implementing it in ministry.

Actively seeking healing suggests that counselors have faced their own pain. One counselor said, "I think it's important for counselors to have experienced their own suffering. Then they can be compassionate and non-judgmental. And they need to remember the healing of the client is not their responsibility, but God's."

3. Spiritual Gifts for Counseling

God has not limited the spiritual gifts for counseling to professionals only. Many, many lay people have been given the gifts of compassion, encouragement, and pastoral counseling. These gifts naturally emerged in childhood and are still evident in adults. Having a heart and giftedness for counseling is an asset for participation in emotional healing ministries. Individuals with these attributes will be the most likely to seek out the opportunity to administer healing prayer to others.

Dr. Trish Treece reports that counselors on her teams, "generally have a heart for counseling ministry and are usually in a reasonable place personally to help others.

They start out being insecure and get surprised by the Lord using them." All counselors can be trained in the steps of the Healing Timeline, but some counselors are naturally gifted and will flourish with the model. They are individuals who over their lifetimes have found themselves repeatedly listening to others' problems and being sought out for advice. These counselors will make good leaders on healing prayer teams. Those with natural counseling gifts will be great contributors to lay ministry and the use of the Healing Timeline.

In the Changepoint Ministry, clients are asked to participate in the counseling process of one other client when they have finished their own individual work. When they have finished their cycle as the client, Changepoint program assigns them to a prayer counseling team. An experienced prayer counselor leads the team and the new member's role may simply be to pray silently. Obviously every client does not have natural gifts for counseling, but God can use every believer in his Kingdom. Natural gifts for counseling are useful, but not required for successfully contributing to the healing of others.

The Client

General guidelines apply when selecting clients who are suitable for the Healing Timeline. The criteria falls into three broad categories:

1. Clients Need to Have a Moderate to High Level of Stability

The Healing Timeline, used by lay and pastoral counselors, is specifically for clients who are generally functioning in their everyday lives but are upset or stressed about a problem. These clients can perform normal functions like going to work, caring for their families, and maintaining personal hygiene. They have at least an average capacity for regulating their emotions and thinking through problems. The Healing Timeline is not for people who are suicidal or in danger of harming themselves. Self-inflicted injury and suicidal ideation conveys an emotional need greater than can be met through the Healing Timeline. These conditions need to be referred to a professional counselor for treatment.

There are many diagnoses that should not be treated by a lay or pastoral counselor with the Healing Timeline. Schizophrenia, untreated bi-polar, manic-depression, eating disorders, multiple personality disorder, severe depression, etc., are outside the application of the Healing Timeline. These diagnoses refer to various levels of a client's instability. The HTL is a very powerful intervention, which can temporarily dysregulate clients. Individuals need a certain level of internal stability to integrate old memories. Healing Timeline sessions can be emotional and clients need to have basic emotional skills for maneuvering through the ups and downs of the timeline repetitions. The level of psychological complexity represented by the diagnoses mentioned here is not treatable with the Healing Timeline. Pastors and prayer counselors might talk or pray with clients who have these conditions, but should not use the Healing Timeline with them.

2. Clients Need the Capacity for Honesty and a Readiness for the Work

In assessing for a client's readiness to receive prayer ministry, one pastor said he looks for clients' willingness to trust that God loves them enough to heal them. This implies they can be honest with God, themselves, and others. Without honesty, the healing prayer sessions will not be effective. When clients give God permission to go wherever he desires to go inside of them, they are opening themselves up to the safest and most accurate detective in existence. If they cannot tolerate the Holy Spirit gently pointing out their erroneous beliefs, bad habits, and buried memories, then they are not ready for the work of the Healing Timeline. Proceeding with clients who are not emotionally ready will be difficult for the counselor and damaging to the client.

A guiding principle for prayer counseling is, "Do not resist resistance." Resistance is the term that refers to a client's reluctance to share appropriate information and follow the counselor's lead. When counselors experience the client blocking their attempts to move the session to a deeper level, it is usually because clients are afraid. If clients cannot move beyond their fear of exposure and defensiveness, then it is probably not the right time for the Healing Timeline. Counselors should not enter into a power struggle with resistant clients. It is better to pray with clients and encourage them, rather than force them to go where they do not want to go with the HTL. At the right time, resistant clients will return and be ready to work on a deeper level.

3. Clients Need to Remember their Lifetime

In order for pastors and lay counselors to successfully use the Healing Timeline, clients must have access to a majority of their memories over their lifetime. It will be frustrating for the client or the counselor to begin the HTL when major time blocks of memories are missing. Memories from certain years are usually missing because the client had something too difficult to process at the time it occurred and the HTL is not sufficient to excavate and heal these memories. Inability to remember certain years is a sign that clients are not ready to receive the Healing Timeline. Occasionally a client will say, "I know something happened when I was eight, but I can't remember my elementary years starting in third grade." Remarks like these indicate that the client has mentally and emotionally separated herself from a memory. This is called dissociation and is not a good match for the Healing Timeline. In order to successfully use the HTL, clients need to have access to a memory for almost every year of their lifetime.

Matching Counselors and Clients

Commonalities surfaced when healing prayer ministries were asked how they match clients to prayer teams. Usually one member of the leadership team functions as the intake coordinator or primary contact for the prayer ministry. In a church or non-profit organization, it is common for this person to be a paid staff person. The designated person usually has a telephone conversation with the prospective client and asks about his or her primary reasons for seeking prayer counseling.

The intake coordinator needs to assess several factors for client readiness to receive the Healing Timeline and explain the policies for the healing prayer ministry.

1. For client readiness, an intake counselor usually asks the client:

> › Why is the client is seeking counseling at

this time? What circumstances have prompted the client to seek healing now?

> Is there a mental health diagnosis or condition from professional therapy? What is the outcome from the client's previous counseling experience?

> What is the client's faith journey and personal relationship to Jesus? Will the client be comfortable with a Christ-centered form of counseling?

> The intake coordinator assesses the overall stability of the client through their conversation. Is the client a good match to the Healing Timeline criteria mentioned above? The best way to insure a good experience for the client and the counselor is to evaluate the suitability of the client for the Healing Timeline.

2. Regarding the ministry policies, an intake coordinator discusses:

> Number of sessions a client can expect. The waiting time before counseling might begin.

> Payment or other obligations in exchange for receiving counseling through the prayer ministry.

> The non-professional status of the prayer ministry. Volunteer prayer ministries stress to clients that they are non-professionals and are providing prayer counseling, not professional therapy.

> The confidentiality policies of the ministry and their obligation to report harmful behaviors or conditions in the client's life.

> Note taking policy of the ministry.

> Some ministries ask clients to sign a form that discusses their policies. Making the expectations clear will help the clients prepare for their prayer counseling.

3. Preparing the timeline and waiting:

In some cases, clients might be asked to prepare the written cue sheet of memories before their first appointment. If this assignment is too difficult or generates too much emotion for clients, they can wait until after their first appointment to discuss the cue sheet with the prayer counseling team. If clients have to wait several weeks or months before their turn to receive prayer counseling, they should be encouraged that God's timing is perfect and he will use the waiting time to prepare for them for healing.

Into the World

The Healing Timeline is God's work and he seems to be spreading the news of this protocol to other parts of the world. Recently a man whose life was changed through a ministry that used the Healing Timeline requested copyright permission to translate the HTL documents into French and the native language of Rwanda. He went to Rwanda planning to lead a building project and teach inner healing prayer, including the Healing Timeline, in the evenings. Circumstances prevented the building materials from arriving in the country. In response, the Rwanda project coordinators gathered sixty native church leaders together for teaching. The week that would have been spent in building was exclusively dedicated to teaching inner healing prayer and the Healing Timeline. The sixty leaders who received the teaching over the week returned to their native villages, including the Congo, to begin using the Healing Timeline in their corners of the world. The Healing Timeline can help adults and children who have been traumatized in war. It appears God is spreading the protocol to reach adults and children throughout the world.

Thirteen

Conclusion

In the process of interviewing counselors who were using the Healing Timeline, one woman shared an experience which underscores the deepest message of this book. She told this story in reference to using the Healing Timeline in her ministry and seeing people set free. Gently awakened early one morning by the Holy Spirit, God said to her, "Mary, I want to give you the keys in this. People are believing lies about themselves and me. I want to tell them the truth. That is the key to the kingdom. That is what will set them free." Mary continued by saying, "With the Healing Timeline we get people connected to the truth," she said. "It's amazing."

Each interview with a prayer counselor or prayer ministry team produced a similar response to the Healing Timeline. "We haven't seen anything like it for helping people believe the truth about themselves," counselors often said. One man continued, "Not only do people believe the truth again, but the lies get erased." Going back into memories and inserting truth into the neural networks gives clients an opportunity to reorder their lives around Jesus' truth. The integration that appears to occur through the timeline seals the truth into the mind and body so freer living naturally follows. Fortunately, with the HTL, clients don't have to work at making positive changes; they are an inevitable outgrowth of believing the truth about God, themselves, and their situations.

The case study, *Lies Versus Truth: Failing in Mathematics*, highlights the power of simply changing beliefs in our hearts. Scotty was naturally gifted in mathematics but in sixth grade had a series of failing marks in math. Jesus said to him in the memory scene, "I made you good at math." Scotty's performance in math changed when he believed Jesus' truth about himself *at the same place* where he had started believing a lie. Imagine how different all our lives would be if Jesus' truth were reinserted where lies had entered our thinking. The Healing Timeline is one way we can fix the broken places in the "pipe of life" and be reconnected to the truth. *The Healing Timeline: God's Shalom for the Past, Present and Future*, gives us a way to go back and erase a lie, rebuilding from a truthful foundation.

The phenomenon of the Healing Timeline is based on the hypothesis that repeated timelines literally change the

brain. When Peggy Pace developed her method of repeating timelines in therapy until a client's distress was gone,
she drew on the current research about the brain. Scientific
understanding today informs us the brain, which was formerly considered fixed, is now clearly found to be plastic,
which means changeable. Much scientific research supports
the concept that influencing the way brain neurons fire will
affect the actual map formed within the brain[1]. Scientists
are able to map patterns of neurons in the brain. When the
stimuli for neural firing is changed consistently over time,
the brain map changes in correlation with the change in
stimuli.

Drawing a hypothesis for the Healing Timeline, we
contend repetitions of a client's timeline, which cause neurons to fire in a repeated pattern throughout the brain, will
also cause neurons to wire together into a new relationship.
In other words, neurons from age six will be rewired to
neurons from age seven, and then to age eight, etc., when
the timeline is repeated enough times to form a connection
between these neurons. We hypothesize new neural pathways are formed from difficult memories into the present.
The outcome for clients is their ability to understand on a
neurological level that their distress is truly over and they
do not have to defend against their emotional wounding
any longer.

Many children grow up in violent, alcoholic, abusive, neglectful, or war-torn environments and carry their

wounding into adulthood. In order to manage in the world, people must find ways to cover up the difficult feelings carried over from childhood. We all develop methods to interface with the outside world while ignoring or managing the internal world. Defense mechanisms or strategies eventually develop to help us manage the turmoil. Even the best strategy, when overused, can keep us out of the flow of life instead of flourishing within it. When clients come for counseling, an automatic childhood strategy is inevitably a major contributor to their difficulties.

Jesus came to set us free. He taught us that his freedom was primarily an internal change in our spirits and minds, which results in a different outward life. The majority of Jesus' miracles occurred within people, not in external circumstances. Personally and collectively, our internal changes by Jesus influence the world. By implementing the Healing Timeline, we also facilitate changing people on the inside. We hypothesize the internal belief and brain structure people carry within themselves changes through the HTL process, which produces outward changes. After the Healing Timeline, people live differently in the world. They can drop their childhood defenses because they know on a biological level their childhood difficulties are over. This allows more of their gifts, talents, and calling to manifest in the world. Christ's light shining within them radiates into more of life.

The first chapter of this book develops the concept

that people's lives could be likened to the rings of a tree. Humans, like trees, are cumulative. Our life experience is stored within the mind, spirit, and body similar to the way a tree lays down a ring for every year. The conditions in which the tree developed are reflected in its rings. So, too, we are highly affected by the conditions in which we develop. Systematically rewiring our "human tree" can shift the way our "rings" are organized and the content held within them. To date we have anecdotal evidence about this process, suggesting the internal changes created by the Healing Timeline are lasting.

Peggy Pace, MA, is the originator of the unique process of changing the brain through repetitions of the timeline. Her method, *Lifespan Integration: Connecting Ego States Through Time*, is taught throughout the US and Europe and is protected by copyright laws. Information about LI can be found at lifespanintegration.com. With Peggy Pace's written authorization, I combined the essential element of her discovery — timeline repetitions — with inner healing prayer. The Healing Timeline was created as a new, Christ-centered modality for helping people around the world gain emotional freedom.

Jesus said he came to "release captives and set free the downtrodden, proclaiming the year of the Lord's favor" (Luke 4:18-21). We participate in his ministry by employing the Healing Timeline to heal the brokenhearted. People wounded in spirit and soul can be rejuvenated by the restoration of truth in their inner beings. The Healing Timeline is one way to integrate truth into our deepest selves.

Timelines heal people. If we did nothing but use timelines, people would get better. Repetitions of the timeline change what people believe about themselves on the inside, which changes their lives on the outside. To repeat a phrase presented throughout the book, "God takes the ghetto out of us and we take ourselves out of the ghetto." All of us carry some aspect of the ghetto inside whether it's our erroneous beliefs, trauma, or our sinful behavior. The Healing Timeline gets the "ghetto" out of people. We, in turn, create a new life without the ghetto.

My hope for this method and book is that it will travel throughout the world. Pastors and prayer counselors can employ the Healing Timeline. It is given for Christian prayer counselors far and wide to begin healing the wounded within their communities. Some conditions pastors and prayer counselors face will be clearly beyond the scope of the Healing Timeline. These conditions need to be referred to professional counselors who have tools beyond the basics outlined here. Although workshops are available in the Healing Timeline, my intent has been to share enough about the method for pastors and Christian lay counselors to employ it by following the directions outlined in this text. The simple process of asking Jesus to lead someone to a hurtful event and healing it through repetitions of their timeline will bring great relief to many. I extend grace and gratitude to the people throughout the world who will heal others with the Healing Timeline. Together, let us take God's shalom into the past, present, and future.

Training
and
Worksops

The Healing Timeline

Since 2005, workshops in *The Healing Timeline: God's Shalom for the Past, Present and Future* have been offered annually in the Seattle, Washington (USA) area. In the workshop, participants practice using the method as well as receive training materials and guidelines. To schedule the Healing Timeline workshop in other areas contact the author at CathyThorpe@msn.com or visit the website: www. HealingTimeline.com.

Lifespan Integration

Mental Health professionals with advanced degrees need the expanded training offered through Lifespan Integration. (LI) This advanced instruction offers tools for successfully treating eating disorders, bi-polar disorder, anxiety, depression, post-traumatic stress disorder, dissociative identity disorder (formerly: multiple personality disorder), and more. It is a secular, mental health modality currently used in the US and Europe. For information about LI contact Peggy Pace at: www.LifeSpanIntegration.com.

Also by
Catherine Thorpe

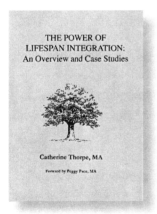

Written for the general public, *The Power of Lifespan Integration: An Overview and Case Studies* describes Peggy Pace's method and its application to various mental health diagnoses. The purpose of the book is to introduce Lifespan Integration to prospective clients and explain its methods and outcomes in easy-to-understand terms. It is also a resource for mental health professionals. A major portion of the book is comprised of case studies on many topics such as depression, trauma, flying anxiety, general anxiety, couples work, LI for children and more. It is currently available at:

www.HealingTimeline.com

247

Chapter One

1. Doidge, Norman: *The Brain that Changes Itself*, Penguin Books, USA 2007.

2. Sandford, John and Paula: *The Transformation of the Inner Man*, p 237. Bridge Publishing Inc., South Plainfield, NJ 1982.

Chapter Three

1. *Time Magazine*, pg. 74, Issue date 1/29/07, Vol. 169, No. 5.

2. Doidge.

3. Doidge, p. 53-54.

4. Begley, Sharon. *Train Your Mind; Change Your Brain*, Ballantine Books, NY 2007. Inside Cover.

5. Amen, Daniel. *Healing ADD: The Breakthrough Program that Allows You to See and Heal the Six Types of ADD*. Berkley Publishing Group, NY 2001.

6. Doidge, p. 54

7. Medina, John. *Brain Rules*, Pear Press, Seattle, WA 2008. p. 54.

8. Siegal, Daniel, MD, lecture, Seattle, WA February, 2003. Author: *The Developing Mind*.

Conclusion

1. Doidge.

Breinigsville, PA USA
22 September 2009
224537BV00005B/2/P